UNAPOLOGETIC OVERSHARING, SELF-AWARENESS, & BUFFALO SAUCE

A BUFFALO SAUCE EVERYWHERE BOOK

By Renata Leo

Edited by Josh Mohs

For me, myself, and I. The person I was, the person I am, and the person I'm becoming.

And to all of you reading this, I hope you can dedicate the work you do along this journey to yourself, too.

CONTENTS

INTRO

AM A HYPOCRITE.

Well, okay not quite a hypocrite, as I won't purport to have all of the answers. I want to state that, while much of this book may contain advice, these are things I'm actually still working on, too.

Like many of those suffering from mental illness, I've spent years going to therapy. It's been everything from enlightening to tearful to trauma-inducing. But as they (all of us who love clichés) say, you get out of therapy what you put into it. And I knew that, as someone trying to work on myself, things were only going to change if I made changes to my internal world. Superficial changes just weren't going to cut it. Any progress I made wouldn't stick if I didn't change something fundamental about myself and how my brain worked.

So I did.

In my work to ultimately become more empathetic, I became a truly self-aware person, so much so that this is one of the first adjectives that people use to describe me. Let me say that again in italics:

I worked so hard on becoming self-aware that even those around me saw the shift and now describe me using the adjective "self-aware."

This self-awareness means a few things:

1. New experiences can be a fucking nightmare. I am constantly checking in with myself about how I feel *so much* that I never get to experience enough to actually, you know, know how I feel.
2. Overall, I get myself. Obviously, I am aware that I will change as a person throughout my life, but I know my patterns fairly well and am open to whatever changes may come.
3. Sometimes, I get frustrated when other people are not as self-aware. I'm not going to lie to you. As empathetic as I've learned to be, sometimes people's lack of self-awareness gets to me. Like, you knew you wouldn't want to do that thing with me. Why did you say yes and then cancel at the last minute?! Dammit!

While this book is all about my journey towards self-awareness, that's not to say that my experience and journey will look exactly like yours (or rather, that my journey looked like yours should you already be self-aware). It won't! Sorry to break it to you, but we're entirely different people! I'm just sharing what has worked for me with the hopes that I can help someone else, too.

So what makes me an expert in all this? The same thing that makes you an expert: a lifetime of experience. I am just your average twenty-something suffering from mental illness and perpetual millennial angst. I am also, however, an expert in me, and becoming an expert in me has been a rewarding experience that I believe helps me every day, even if the dark cloud of depression is looming over me.

Now, when I say "millennial angst," I am referring to dealing with the stresses of the modern person coming-of-age. I'm talking about being told that only college can lead to a good job, then drowning yourself in student loan debt; coming of age in a world that is only starting to be more open about acknowledging and discussing mental illnesses; never feeling like you're doing enough when there are "so many opportunities" available to you; and having strangers on the internet tell you that they have it worse, so you shouldn't be complaining. These problems can happen to anyone at any age, of course, but these are some of the things that have been deemed a part of the "quintessential millennial experience."

But if we're all experts, then why the hell am I here talking about this? Well, dear reader, I *love* writing. I seriously love writing. I'm that person from your English class who was pondering prepositions and thinking about translation and assessing alliterations. I was the kid in middle school who not only had a notebook full of poetry, but also a hard drive full of fiction. Now, those are things I may never share because they were pretty terrible, but I did them because I just enjoy writing! All throughout my therapy journey and beyond, I kept up a blog where I wrote all about the new things that I discovered about myself as well as the misadventures that I'd had along the way. I guess I'd always hoped that my thoughts would make other people feel less alone. And so now, I hope that for you. I hope that you read this and see yourself in this book. I hope you laugh, even if it's through tears.

The journey into self-awareness isn't always easy and self-awareness doesn't mean that you will automatically love yourself, either. Hell, becoming self-aware also means facing all of the things that you *don't* like about yourself. But of course, you can't really love someone unless you know them. So self-awareness is an important facet that can get you part of the way there. At least, it did for me.

Even if you don't love yourself right away, you can still stand up for yourself unapologetically. I don't know about you, but I say "I'm sorry" a lot, even when it's unnecessary. I apologize for literally everything from doing something that I've never done before incorrectly to asking a totally valid and warranted question. I've had friends, managers, partners, life coaches, and my aforementioned therapist tell me that. It's just a word I say as a reflex. Armed with the knowledge of myself and my personality, I am striving to be far less apologetic about who I am because I can explain where my impulses come from. Instead of apologizing for who I am, I am working instead on going into details about why I feel a certain way or wax poetic about all my feelings on a particular topic. In this area of my life, I don't want it to be an "I'm sorry," but rather a "let me explain." And that can make all the difference.

In this book (my first, yay!), I'm going to outline what I've discovered in my journey to becoming self-aware. I'll talk about past habits that I realized don't serve me, some preconceived notions that have harmed me, and why I think being yourself is an awesome fucking thing to be. I'll share with you all of those little "eureka" moments that I've had in my life that have shaped me into the person I am today, and hopefully, in turn, that will spark a bit of self-acceptance curiosity in you. Maybe a bit of "hey, I've never thought of it that way!" Or a sprinkling of "wow, I should show myself more compassion." Possibly even a smattering of "damn, I'm pretty freaking cool!"

I know what you're thinking "I'm self-aware, already; I don't need your silly advice in your silly book with your silly clichés, Renata!"

Well, my first thought is...that's hurtful! If you don't have anything nice to say, don't say anything at all!

My next thought is that I know that! No one *needs* this book. I may be a truly terrible salesperson, but I really believe that no one needs cheesy self-help books to do anything. While our external world and circumstances shape much of our lives, nothing external can change without changing our internal worlds. Changing your internal world takes skill and self-awareness. You don't actually need anyone else to do that. But, if you'd like to read a book by someone personable who has already done it and wants to hold your hand through it, I'm here for you.

Also, I promise you that there will be some funny stuff in this book. I'd like to think that purchasing and reading this book will help everyone, if for no other reason than to give you a chuckle or a chortle or a giggle or maybe even a belly laugh. I'm aiming high here.

GROUND RULES FOR THIS BOOK:

- Here is your big ol' TRIGGER WARNING: I talk a lot about mental illness in this book. Namely: depression, anxiety, and some eating disorder stuff, too. If you find content about those topics especially triggering, please stop here! I have no interest in harming anyone or their mental health.

- Although this book addresses my journey with mental health, I am NOT a mental health professional. This book is advice from a human suffering from mental illness and describes what has worked for me. The advice in this book is not recommended as treatment for any mental illness or as a replacement for any treatment options. In fact, I am quite fond of therapy and would recommend therapy to anyone and everyone!

- If, anywhere in this book, I seem braggadocious, I want you to read the passage again and sit with that assumption. What made you feel that way? Could it be that I openly stated that I'm good at something in a factual way? *Gasp! So unabashed!* I endeavor to be as open and honest as possible with you in this book, which means claiming my entire experience, my successes and my shortcomings. After all, the goal here is to be yourself and not apologize – that means you have to recognize the good in yourself as well as the bad. I'm great at some things, that's just a fact. You are, too!

- I write the way that I speak, which means that there will be cursing in this book. If you are not a fan of colorful language, this colorful fucking book is probably not for you.
- I am going to state right here and now that I come from a place of privilege. While my story does involve struggling with mental illness and what I have defined above as "millennial angst," I have never had to overcome the awful experiences like poverty and racism that are a reality for so many.
- Worksheets! This book has them! There is a worksheet after every chapter to help you apply what you've just read. I've also provided examples on the worksheets to hopefully help you get the ball rolling. Sit with the worksheet questions for a bit before answering if you need to, but when in doubt, don't think too hard! Just write the first thing that comes to mind and go from there. Sometimes, you just need to get some thoughts down on paper in order for inspiration to start flowing. While I do believe that the worksheets can help the theoretical concepts become more concrete, if you're not a worksheet person, no worries! Just skip over each worksheet and jump into the next chapter. I won't tell you how to live your life!
- I make a lot of cheesy jokes. A lot. I hope they're gouda, I'm not a muenster.
- Here, like on my blog, we get two things straight right off the bat: pants are the worst, and Buffalo sauce is the best. Yes, these are hills I am willing to die on.
- The most important rule of this book: don't be so hard on yourself! Reading this might get you caught in the mental

trap of wanting to be a different person right away or disliking your current habits. But there's nothing wrong with you! If there's anything you want to change about yourself, there's plenty of time, but growth doesn't come from shame and guilt. It comes from love and understanding. Don't be hard on yourself...you're doing just fine.

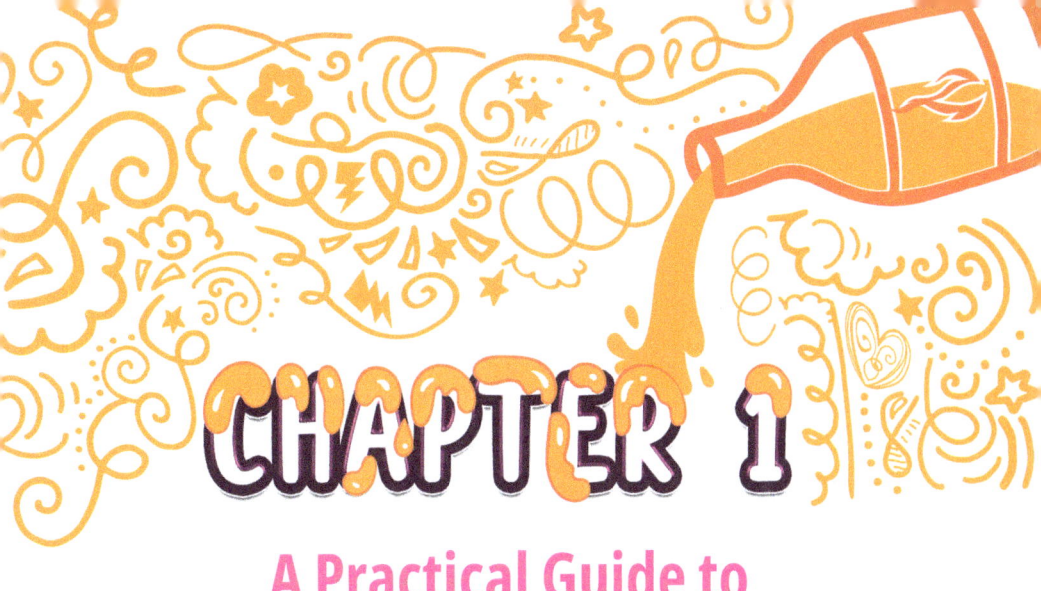

CHAPTER 1

A Practical Guide to Understanding Yourself

LEARNING YOUR PATTERNS

I don't know about you, but I love personality quizzes. Whether I'm taking the Myers-Briggs or a test that tells me what kind of french fry I am (#curlyorbust), I love to see the results and what they say about me. I like to plug all of my patterns into a quiz and see what the culmination of all of those patterns amounts to. And as a general rule, those results don't surprise me one bit. As a self-aware person with an inclination for noticing patterns and after years of living inside this mind and body,

I have certain expectations when it comes to my personality and my reactions.

A while ago, I had plans with a friend from my old job. I'd had a busy day, but the extrovert in me was happy to make time to see her. I went test-driving cars in the morning, stopped at the jewelry store to pick up something for my mom, and stopped at my grandparents' house. I calculated how much time I had in order to get home to see my friend. If I only stayed an hour at my grandparents' house, I'd be home in plenty of time. Perfect.

Of course, as soon as I walked into my grandparents' house, they offered to stuff me full of bacon and waffles (like grandparents do). I always text this friend frequently throughout the day, so I texted her that I was with my grandparents getting fed. I just thought it would be a funny text. "LOL of course they had to offer me food!"

Unfortunately, she took my text as me saying that I wouldn't have time to see her. My stomach bottomed out and that feeling of impending doom that only comes with plans falling through began to set in. I texted her when I left my grandparents' house an hour later and told her when I'd be home. I was already starting to spiral thinking that our visit was falling apart.

As I started to become more and more upset, there were several other lapses in our communication that ended up with her not coming over. At the end of the day, we talked it out and realized that it was a big misunderstanding, but I couldn't understand why it bothered me so much.

It didn't take me too long to realize that the reason I was allowing this miscommunication to bother me was the fact that this issue was bumping up against my core values.

I've worked with several life coaches throughout the past few years, and they have all taught me some valuable lessons about myself. Years ago, when I started with my first life coach, she had me write out all of my core values. Unsurprisingly, many were about people and connection. Being responsible was one of them, which was also unsurprising considering the fact that I've always been so fucking proud to be an overly responsible stickler. And, of course, self-awareness was also high on the list.

This coach then tasked me with paying attention when something really bothers me and figuring out why it bothers me. She told me to go through my core values and see if I was bothered because what was happening went against them. As I started thinking about the things that had bothered me recently, I realized that, on the whole, she was right. Every time something bothered me, it often went against my values. Feeling like I wasn't very self-aware, feeling like I didn't belong, feeling like I wasn't being empathetic – they all caused an emotional reaction because they made me feel as though I wasn't living out my core values. Even though I don't work with that life coach anymore, I still use this technique whenever I get that nagging feeling that something is upsetting me far more than it should.

The recent issue with my friend highlighted this again for me. Although this was an absolute misunderstanding, my brain had decided that my friend was indirectly implying that I didn't schedule my time properly. I worried that I was being seen as irresponsible and an unreliable friend, directly contradicting two values that I hold at the very core of my being. The benefit of understanding where these feelings come from is being able to combat them. In this example, now that I know that I was so upset because I felt like I was being called irresponsible, I can talk myself back down. She wasn't implying that I was an irresponsible person, it was just a misunderstanding. I repeat, I am not an irresponsible person. It was just a misunderstanding. And the next time something like this arises, I can think more rationally and keep my cool without getting as upset.

This exercise in figuring out my core values taught me a lot about my personal patterns and the driving forces behind them. I have found understanding my patterns to be paramount in understanding myself. After all, patterns don't only show us the past, but they help us to predict the future as well. My patterns help me to see when something is going right or wrong.

UNDERSTANDING YOUR PATTERNS

As a high-functioning person with mental illness, sometimes depression, anxiety, and disordered eating episodes can sneak up on me without me even realizing. Suddenly, I'm falling asleep an hour earlier, I'm abandoning even the parts of my routine that I like, and I'm unable to handle more than sleeping, eating, and doing my 9-to-5 job. Recognizing these small patterns that appear when I'm in the throes of depression can help me get ahead of it and allow me to give myself grace about what I can and can't handle.

After years of cycling motivation, depression, and energy, I began to realize that my patterns resemble a theory I learned about in my psychology courses in college: Maslow's Hierarchy of needs. Maslow theorized that there's a hierarchy of human needs and that basic physiological needs have to be met before more complex psychological needs even make themselves known. At the bottom, you have food, shelter, physical wellness, etc., while higher up, you have things like community and happiness.

I find that tooth pain shows this theory particularly acutely. Can you focus on literally *anything fucking else* when your teeth are in pain? No, right? That's because your most basic needs aren't being met!

So one day, I sat down and created "Renata's Hierarchy of Needs" (or as I like to sometimes call it, Mas-Leo's Hierarchy of needs) where I defined for myself what my different levels were. I sat back and reflected on the different levels of motivation and energy that I've had in the past, and I used that information to create the levels on my pyramid and recognize what I can handle at different times.

This is my handy dandy "Hierarchy of Needs." I have 5 different levels that show how much I can handle in my different mental and emotional states.

Like Maslow's Hierarchy of Needs, the bottom rung consists of my basic needs. If those aren't met, I can't focus on much else, and other needs don't even make themselves known. As my state improves more and more, I can handle more, too! I have outlined my levels below so that you can understand exactly what I was thinking when I created them.

LOWEST RUNG: BASIC NEEDS

Here's where all the things I need to survive come in. Physical wellness, food, shelter, etc. – everything that I need to actually live. When these things are disrupted (pain, no sleep, starving, dehydrated), it's hard to focus on anything else. Sorry depression, you'll have to wait. I need a root canal and a donut, ASAP.

2ND RUNG: PSYCHOLOGICAL HEALTH

This is where my emotional and mental health start to come into play. While I am physically able to function, I'm in such emotional distress that I'm not able to actually do many human activities. Basic tasks like brushing my teeth are overwhelming. The thought of making a full meal is exhausting, so I am only having snacks for my meals. I may be taking breaks in my day to have an emotional outburst or just to breathe so that I can function. Any sort of interaction fills me with anxiety, so I don't reach out to anyone for support. If I am able to interact with anyone, I have a set of what I call "canned answers" that normal humans tend to use when interacting. "Cool." "Yeah, I feel you." "Everything is the fucking worst." Subsequently, I assume that everyone thinks I'm too boring to talk to anyway!

3RD RUNG: PRE-EXISTING RELATIONSHIPS AND PROJECTS

Once I pass the previous rung and don't feel like I'm a drain on those around me, I start craving interaction. At the same time, on this lower rung, I'm still only able to interact successfully with those in my inner circle. I'm going to need more energy to build foundations for new relationships or exchange pleasantries with acquaintances. When I'm mentally well enough to rely on others and have them rely on me, I feel most fulfilled when I'm engaging and relying on those support systems. While alone, I'm able to focus on my hobbies and interests, but only if they're familiar (redoing puzzles I've already done, rewatching shows I've already watched, rereading books I've already read, etc.). On this rung, I've also graduated to being able to complete more complicated tasks, so I'm finally able to cook myself some actual meals. I then have the energy to pick back up one or two of the projects that I've been neglecting while on the lower rungs struggling to function. But like with my relationships, I'm still not comfortable enough to start new projects, just to work on those I had already started.

4TH RUNG: NEW NON-ANXIETY-INDUCING EXPERIENCES

On this rung, I am comfortable enough with my mental health and all of my current projects that I can start taking on new ones! The caveat here is that I'm still not confident and well enough to take on *unpredictable* projects. If I know that I can complete this new project well, that I will be comfortable with every stage of the new project, and/or that I've done something similar before, I can start a new project at this stage. Hell, this is the stage where I can start absorbing new media, too. New shows, music, and podcasts can all happen at this stage because I'm okay with a little bit of uncertainty, just not a lot of it. On the social side of things, I can venture out a bit, too, and attend social gatherings with a fair amount of comfort. Being in crowded places is not as intimidating, as long as I have a buddy!

TOP RUNG: INTO THE UNKNOWN

At this stage, it's really anything goes. I have the confidence to try new things, even if they seem scary. I am able to take leaps of faith and believe in myself in ways that I haven't before. I'm comfortable enough in my abilities to think: "well, I know I can handle 30% of this, I'll just figure out the rest later!" Not only that, but I'm giving myself grace when I struggle to figure out what I don't know. Doesn't this rung sound great? Good mental health, energy to start new things, and stellar confidence? Sounds like living the dream to me!

Great news! I've made it easy for you to make your own! On the worksheet that follows this chapter, you can make your own hierarchy of needs. There's a blank pyramid as well as my own explanations of the levels to help you create your own.

Of course, the trick then is to know which level you're on at any given time and recognize the limitations of that level. Not knowing what you can and can't handle can be challenging for several reasons, not only for you but for the people around you. If you think you can handle taking on 5 extra activities on one particular week, but you're actually having a breakdown every time you imagine doing more than 2 extra activities, you may commit to things that you don't have the energy for and let someone down by either bailing at the last second or just not being fully present when the activity is taking place. Figuring out what you can and can't handle becomes an exercise in learning how to say "no."

SAY "NO" EVERY ONCE IN A WHILE!

I do recognize that saying "no" isn't always easy. There's a lot of societal pressure to say "yes" to things so that you aren't letting people down, aren't being confrontational, don't seem too sensitive, are being social enough to fit in with a group...the list goes on and on. Hell, we even have an acronym for Fear of Missing Out!

I knew that I wanted to fully understand what my different levels of need and energy were so that I could properly gauge what I should be saying "yes" and "no" to. For me, in order to know how much I can handle in any given amount of time, I needed to find out how much was too much. This wasn't particularly challenging for me, considering my propensity for taking on WAY too many projects at once. When committing to something, I try to use previous experience to see how many days I can hustle without rest and how much energy I'll need for any given activity.

Everyone is different in this area, too. What might be too much for me isn't too much for someone else. I've had to learn in my journey towards becoming more empathetic that the number of things that any one person can handle is not universal. This not only means that I need to be understanding of friends who need more alone time, but I also need to surround myself with people who are understanding of me and my energy. I'm still working on learning exactly how much downtime I need in order to not feel overwhelmed, and I'm trying my best not to commit to too much when I know that I'm not able to handle it.

More importantly, I'm also learning how to say "no" to anything that I know deep down I won't want to do anyway. I've spent so many years agreeing to things that I knew I didn't want to do because I thought I could convince myself when the time came that I would actually want to do them. I do the same thing when I am presented with opportunities to take on more projects. Not only do I not have time to do all the things, but there are some things that I just don't *want* to do. The relentlessly ambitious Renata may want to try to do everything that looks good on a resume and will teach her new skills, but she just literally can't.

Beyond physical limitations, I don't even *want* to do all the things. Even if there's an experience that would teach me something new, I may just not enjoy it, and that's okay. In college, I became the president of a club because I thought it would look good on my resume, not because I really wanted to do it. I hated it and sucked at it because it just wasn't what I wanted to do. I'd rather be upfront and tell someone that I don't want to do something or just decide to bypass opportunities right off the bat instead of bailing or hating my life, but that wasn't possible until I learned how to be comfortable saying "no." I consider it to be Marie Kondo-ing my life in a way, but instead of clearing out the *stuff* that doesn't bring me joy, I'm clearing out the *activities* that don't bring me joy.

Think back to the last time you bailed on something halfway through. Was it something you knew that you wouldn't want to do? Something you would've preferred to say "no" to in the first place?

USING YOUR PATTERNS TO FIGURE OUT WHAT TO SAY "NO" TO

When I interviewed at graduate schools, I was very careful with my energy. They always had back-to-back optional events for the interviewees throughout the process, and I tried to figure out exactly how many activities I could handle and how many I should skip. Plenty of nights were spent home alone with just my student host, and honestly, those nights were more fun to me than hanging out with a big group. I was grateful to just spend the time getting to know my host really well and conserving my energy for my interviews. Don't get me wrong. By my third school visit, I was crying on the phone with my mom that I wanted to be home, but without recognizing that I needed some me time and to say "no" to some of the events, I would have burnt out much sooner.

Interviewing at graduate schools also helped me to recognize when things aren't right for me according to my patterns.

When I attended undergrad, I fell in love with Student Affairs. I worked in several different offices on campus, and I was bitten by the bug. The helping-college-students-for-a-living beetle (yeah, okay, so that's not a thing, but it's already been typed, so I'm going with it). As a college student who really struggled to acclimate, it was so rewarding to have the opportunity to help other students feel comfortable on campus. By the end of my senior year, I knew that I wanted to do this for a living.

For several reasons and life circumstances, my plans to get my degree in Student Affairs were postponed, but I revisited the idea and did more and more research every year until my mentor back at my undergraduate college said:

"Renata, can I be frank?" (This is where I resisted the urge to tell her that her name is Annie, but she can be Frank if she wants to...please don't hate me) "You've been toying with this idea for years now. It's time to go to grad school."

And so, to grad school I went. Well, to grad school *interviews* I went.

I argued with Annie over how many schools I should apply to and how many to visit for interviews (on both decisions we compromised – for example, she wanted me to apply to 5 and I wanted to apply to 23, so we settled on 6). I was excited to finally have my plans underway.

In the end, I visited 4 different schools around the country, had wicked jet lag while staying in the same time zone, cried for home several times, and visited a variety of Targets.

Throughout every single visit, I was listening closely to every professor and department head talk about Student Affairs and about how much of yourself you have to give in that career. I texted one of my friends several times for reassurance, and he (as he had many times before) assured me that I could be successful in this field and that I would really truly enjoy it.

And while I was actually starting to doubt that, I couldn't let go of the dream. I was just self-sabotaging, I told myself.

Hell, at one point, I talked to another potential student about needing time to take care of myself, and her response was to scoff and ask, "Are you sure you want to go into Student Affairs?" "Yes!" I immediately thought, enthusiastically. I had wanted that for three long years.

My last visit was to the University of South Carolina. I was going in confident – I had already had an excellent offer from my top choice school and I was flying in on my birthday, so I had a free birthday dessert wherever we went for dinner to look forward to. I was sitting pretty.

On the first full day of activities, the head of the department spoke. Same story, different day. Ambitious students, passionate, overworked professionals, the usual. But something had changed inside me. Something had opened me up to really listening to the words. I looked around the room at all of the other future Student Affairs professionals, and they were the epitome of everything that every speaker at every school was saying. Not only were they looking to improve the lives of students (which was my main goal), but they were also enthusiastically chattering about conferences and seminars. For them, Student Affairs wasn't just their *livelihood*, it was their *lives*.

Until this moment, I hadn't considered this to be problematic. So what if everyone was more excited and passionate than me? I could work in Student Affairs and be one of those people who isn't the most enthusiastic in the room.

But that's just not who I am.

As someone who is almost always one of the most energetic and passionate people in the room, I realized that I was not doing what was right for me. I had been avoiding thinking about the fact that while everyone else was so ready to dive in and make Student Affairs their everything, I had spent the past several years working on my own work/life balance. I had been avoiding the fact that I was not as passionate as everyone else, and that just *wasn't me*. My eyes were finally opening, and I was realizing that this wasn't my path.

I texted my ex/bestie/editor freaking out (about this situation in particular) one final time. My future plans were crumbling before me, but I felt a sense of relief at typing to him that I didn't think I was making the right choice for myself and my life. As someone who knows me better than anyone else, Josh's words helped me to fully accept this decision that was a long time coming: I wasn't going to graduate school.

"You seem so at peace about this."

For me, at least, the moral of this story is to not get so caught up in one singular goal that you lose sight of what you really want. The universe, or your gut, or God, or whoever you believe in is sending you signs every day. Sometimes they're small, like a song stuck in your head, but other times, they're big like WHAT ARE YOU FUCKING DOING!? YOU WON'T LIKE GRADUATE SCHOOL!!!

Don't put those blinders on, put your head down, and ignore the signs. Having some direction and some definitive goals may seem really tempting, but don't let that succubus of security tempt you into doing something that you actually wouldn't enjoy.

With those blinders up, I was unable to see something that is *so clear* to me now looking back: I wasn't myself in those interviews. I have always had an enthusiastic and obsessive personality, but everyone around me was far more enthusiastic about Student Affairs than I was. I should have known that this wasn't for me when I was one of the least enthusiastic people in the room. That's just not me.

This is literally how I approach everything in my life: get super excited about something and obsess about it repeatedly, then deal with reality later. And because I'm an extrovert who basically needs to tell everyone around me everything about me in order to survive, I love to share the things I'm excited about (although I've had to work on swallowing my pride in order to be vulnerable enough to share about opportunities I might not get!).

I can't tell you how many freelancing opportunities that I've gotten, namely because of my enthusiasm. When I'm excited about something, I wear it plainly on my face and word it plainly in my writing. I let my passion shine through and become obsessed in the best possible way. Hell, I usually tell my freelance clients that it will take me several days or weeks to get something done since I have a full-time job, but usually, I just complete the job within a matter of hours, because I'm just too excited to wait!

In fact, I have a bad habit of overlooking the bad parts of things because I'm so excited about the good facets (hence going through undergrad as a Neuroscience major with the intention of becoming a genetic researcher or applying to graduate school even though deep down, I knew that research wasn't for me). I got my life coaching certification last year and yet again, I completely put up my blinders and ignored everything that I wouldn't like about coaching. Sure, I've never wanted to build my own business, but I'm helping people! Yeah, I hate randos approaching me on the internet, but I'll get over that! Wow, do I hate marketing myself, but you know you can't enjoy everything about what you do!

I completely ignored all the signs that I *shouldn't* start my own coaching practice until I was in a full panic spiral and rethinking my entire life. At the end of the day, I'm glad that I got my certification, and I learned a lot from it, but I realistically knew the entire time that I didn't want to build my own business. I just ignored the signs instead of listening to my gut.

For undergrad, graduate school and creating a coaching business, the way that I realized that they weren't for me was my relative lack of enthusiasm. While I was somewhat excited, the people around me seemed to be over the moon. When I was in undergrad studying Neuroscience, the other people in my major kept talking about internships and research presentations. When I went to interview at graduate schools, people kept talking about all these conferences to make them better professionals. As an entrepreneur, other entrepreneurs kept excitedly talking about creating and taking different courses and resources to make more money and better their businesses. When those around me are so much more excited than I am, I know that it's time to step back and reassess. Enthusiasm is what I'm all about. Hell, one of my main Enneagram types is "The Enthusiast" (I told you I liked personality quizzes). My comfort zone is being the super enthusiastic one in the room – it's a red flag to me if everyone else is excited and I'm indifferent.

But it can take me forever to realize how unenthusiastic I am about certain things. I just get so pumped about the good things and get swept up in my visions of an awesome future. I like to compare my enthusiastic nature to that of a sea sponge who is very near and dear to me, Spongebob Squarepants. He was a big part of my childhood, after all, but many people have called out his personality flaw of overly romanticizing things to the point where he legitimately thinks that everything will go exactly as he imagines, and therefore finds himself completely crashing when something doesn't go as he anticipated. I can absolutely relate. Honestly though, there are worse traits to have.

The only reason that this sometimes bites me in the ass is my all-or-nothing personality. When you see things in black and white, you can have a hard time remembering that you can feel differently about different facets of the same thing. Once I realized that I didn't want to build a coaching business, I wanted to distance myself as much as I could from coaching. Seeing other coaches promoting themselves on Facebook made me cringe and I had to take a break from giving sample coaching sessions because I just can't be partially into something. I need to have both feet in or neither. I just *need* to be overly enthusiastic to be able to do something.

Enthusiasm and dreaming of the future are who I am. While I recognize that it can leave me crashing down from dreaming too big, I would still rather have the big dreams in the first place. To paraphrase Shakespeare, "'Tis better to have dreamed big and had all of your hopes and dreams come crashing down on you than never to have dreamed at all."

Knowing yourself can save you from committing to many things that would ultimately make you feel unhappy. Understanding your patterns and listening to your internal voice is how you can avoid doing things that you don't want to do or won't have the energy for. Sometimes in life, doing things that we don't like are unavoidable. There are parts of our days that are unpleasant. Maybe you dislike doing laundry. Maybe your daily 9 am meetings aren't your thing. We will always have to face unpleasantness. However, I've found that there is a difference between doing things that I dislike but have to do anyway, and doing things that I actively dread doing that I'm just forcing myself to do. While dislike is something that everyone has to put up with every once in a while, dread, for me, is something that makes life not worth living. Dread is a sign that something needs to change.

WHEN SAYING "NO" IS NO LONGER OPTIONAL, BUT NECESSARY

I learned the difference between dislike and dread when I was graduating from college and choosing my future career path. I went to college to become a research scientist. I spent my entire college career ignoring what I did not like about research. I dreaded each lab and each research paper, and I even sobbed hysterically during one of our animal lab procedures. I kept making all kinds of excuses as to why I could still enjoy research. No job is perfect, after all, and I wouldn't love every part of anything. It wasn't until I understood that I could, and even *should*, say "no" to becoming a researcher that I realized how much I dreaded pretty much everything about research. While I had decided years previously that I would go into research, it was okay to change my course and do something else because research would make me profoundly unhappy.

My blindly diving into academia wasn't over after my undergraduate career, as you know. When I decided to go back to school to get my degree in Student Affairs, I spent countless hours applying to and interviewing at schools, psyching myself up the entire time. Sure, I wouldn't enjoy the schoolwork, but that was okay. Sure, I wasn't nearly as excited about conferences and professional growth as my peers, no big deal. Sure, I doubted I would enjoy working in Student Affairs as an administrator as opposed to a student, but so what? I would just have to get the hell over it. It wasn't until I really considered the fact that I shouldn't dread all of these things about my professional life that I was able to take away the blinders and make a realistic decision as to what would actually make me happy.

When it comes to our livelihoods, it's important to find something we're at least somewhat happy with. When you're spending at least a third of your day at work, you can't wake up dreading every single day. You don't have to look forward to every single day and every single aspect of your job, but dreading getting out of bed every morning is a terrible feeling that no one should have to experience. I'm striving to be as transparent with my bosses as possible. If there are projects I'm dreading, I make sure they know my feelings. Don't get me wrong, I would never complain constantly, but I've found it's best to be honest with your boss about your strengths, weaknesses, and happiness. Every boss wants their employees performing optimally, and no one is performing optimally if they're dreading coming into work.

For me, this learning experience wasn't just about being happy in my career. There have been so many hobbies/clubs/organizations that I've had in my life which I continued participating in even though I dreaded doing them. If you're dreading doing something and it isn't necessary for the health and wellbeing of yourself or those around you, here is the sign you've been looking for: CUT. IT. OUT. Seriously, it can feel like a big deal to just completely drop something you've been doing for a while, but if you're dreading it, then you will be living a better life once it is gone. Just imagine getting rid of it and replacing it with something you love doing. Don't you feel better already?

I personally grew up around a lot of influences that said quitting anything was despicable and that you really need to stick with things and persevere for some strange and unnecessary reason. As an adult, it's been hard to break out of this mindset and realize leaving something behind that isn't serving you isn't only good, but necessary! We only have one life to live here, and there's no point in spending your time doing things you dread.

This can even mean standing up to or cutting off toxic people or people that you've simply outgrown. As kids, we can be too afraid to stand up for ourselves for fear of not fitting in or being seen as too sensitive or too mean. As adults who have matured (at least a bit, hopefully), we can more realistically assess how we're treated and demand to be treated correctly. Like everything else, it's okay to dislike people and not mesh with them perfectly, but if you're dreading seeing them, it could be time to reflect and move on. There's no shame in distancing yourself from people who make you feel bad. Protecting your energy and putting yourself first is important, even if it means cutting out people who you've known for a long time.

I'm sure I'm not the only one with a lot of feelings about... everything. There's only so much control we have over what we face in life and how much of it we enjoy. There are plenty of things that we dislike and even dread, but the best thing that we can do is carefully exercise the control we have over this life. Unpleasantness is inevitable, but dread can be avoidable. Take a step back and see how you feel. If you find that there's something in life that you dread, see if you can find a way around it. Unfortunately, there is a possibility that you're in a place where you can't avoid dread. If the "basic needs" rung on your hierarchy isn't being met because you don't have decent health, food, shelter, etc, you won't be able to advance through the rungs and leave a job that you dread. If this is your situation, I'm very sorry and hope that it improves and that you can ditch the dread soon. You're not actually living your life if all that you're feeling is dread.

Sometimes, we can get caught up in things that we dread because we feel we "should" continue to do things that we've committed to, even if we've realized that they're not for us or if we've outgrown them. Think about the last hobby that you took on or the last commitment you made that made you feel dread. Didn't you feel relieved when that commitment was over or when you were able to abandon that hobby? That's because feeling regular dread is no way to live life! We must learn to completely abandon the idea that "shoulds" rule our lives in order to live a happy and fulfilled life.

But before we dive into the evil that is "shoulds," I promised you a worksheet! It's time to make your own hierarchy of needs!

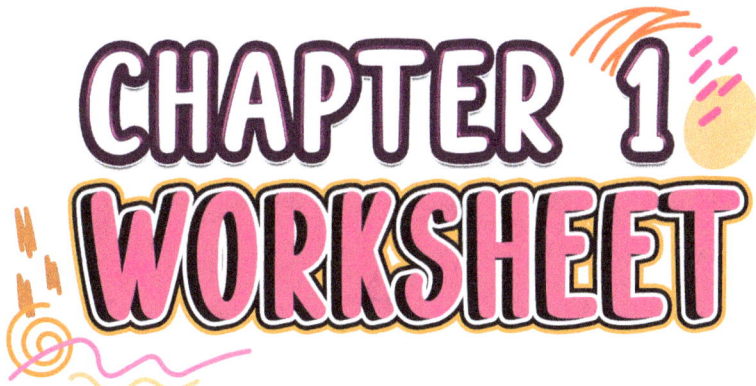

CHAPTER 1 WORKSHEET

Creating my own hierarchy of needs has been incredibly helpful for me to give myself grace when I can't handle quite as much as I expect from myself. Sure, at my best I can work on 6 projects at once, but towards the bottom, I'm barely able to complete my 9-to-5 job. I am now able to recognize when I'm on those lower rungs and choose not to take on more projects for my mental health.

Maybe this technique can help you, too!

At the bottom of this sheet, there's a blank pyramid for you to fill out. You can have as many levels as you want! Is 5 too many? Make fewer! Is 5 too few? Make more! Just as long as you're doing some self-reflection, you're doing it right.

Make sense?

Will your pyramid look similar to mine or totally different? Fill out the pyramid below with your personal levels!

RUNG 1:

Basic needs: These are my basic needs (physical wellness, food, shelter, etc).

_____

_____

_____

_____

_____

RUNG 2:

Psychological Health: On this rung, I am physically well enough to function, however, I am in emotional distress and struggling with basic tasks and social interaction.

_____

_____

_____

_____

_____

RUNG 3:

Pre-Existing Relationships and Projects: Here, my emotional/mental health are such that I can be social and revisit pre-existing projects.

_____

_____

_____

_____

_____

RUNG 4:

New Non-Anxiety-Inducing Experiences: On this rung, I'm able to actually start some new hobbies and projects, engage with new media and start being more social as long as I already feel somewhat comfortable with them.

_____

_____

_____

_____

_____

RUNG 5:

Into the Unknown: I am thriving. Not only can I take on new things, but I am comfortable trying things I've never tried before.

_____

_____

_____

_____

_____

I MADE MORE RUNGS, GIVE ME MORE SPACE!

Okay, fine! Here's more space, sassypants!

_____

_____

_____

_____

_____

_____

Self-Compassion Time!

Sit with your pyramid. Think about a time in your life when you felt like you should be getting more things done, but just found yourself unable to live up to your own standards.

Were you on a lower rung of your pyramid at that time? Were you not having enough of your basic needs met in order to transcend to a higher rung to handle more responsibility and effort?

Promise yourself that next time you're on that lower rung, you'll allow yourself to exist there for as long as you need and figure out *what you need* to move up the pyramid.

CHAPTER 2

Kicking "Shoulds" to the Curb

NOW THAT YOU KNOW what your levels are (and they may change at some point), you can be better prepared to give yourself grace and realize that you don't have to be able to do everything you feel you *should* do all the time. Maybe it's time to adjust your expectations of yourself.

In fact, maybe it's time we throw out "should" altogether...

"SHOULDS" RUIN EVERYTHING!

Being comfortable creating needless goals for myself, I have almost always created needless boundaries as well. If I didn't like Hilary Duff, I couldn't allow myself to engage with any of her projects. If someone had presumably wronged me in some way, I'd cut them off without even giving them the chance to explain themselves, mistakes or not. If I decided that I didn't think leggings should be worn as pants, I would judge anyone who wore them as pants and vow never to wear anything less casual than jeans.

Back in high school, I remember one of my friends hearing some of my personal "rules" and looking at me astounded.

"Those sound restrictive."

That's because they were! I liked to restrict myself. It felt safer and my rules helped me dictate how I should feel. Didn't everyone have restrictive personal rules to keep them in line?

In college, while studying abroad in Spain, I had a friend who opened up my worldview a bit more. While a group of us was sitting around talking about our governing rules, she responded, "I don't think there really are any rules besides 'You Do You.'"

You may think this is a thinly veiled attempt to brag about how many friends I have. And you might be right.

But I also want to point out that this shook me to my core. I do me? *I do me?* I DO ME?! This flagrantly ignored all the useless boundaries that I had created for myself. I just do what I want to do? But where are all the "shoulds" that make me so comfortable?

In reality though, this is true. For the most part, should doesn't really exist. Yup, you read that correctly.

Should.

Doesn't.

Exist.

Now, first of all, I want to point out that there are shoulds in the sense of hurting or neglecting yourself or others. You should eat food because you need nourishment. You shouldn't manipulate your partner just to hurt them. I do believe that we should go throughout life causing as little harm as possible.

But other than that...

We spend far too much time and energy questioning our "shoulds." Ads telling you how you should workout and eat and look. Family members telling you how you should act. TV shows and media telling you how you should feel and respond to certain situations. You can even find this across the internet on chat forums. People constantly try to understand the should of what they're doing or how they think and feel. "Am I normal for thinking this way?"

People want to fit in. Of course they do. They want to know that their feelings and actions are seen as normal. They want to understand what they should be doing so that they can feel safe and secure and justified. Shoulds give us direction.

Shoulds cause strangers on the internet to comment on everyone else's life and critique it. They believe in shoulds and think their shoulds are the right shoulds.

Sometimes, we get so caught up in the shoulds, that we live in our heads and forget to live our lives!

I think it's time we kicked should to the curb and adopt the "you do you" mentality. I don't know about you, but I'm sick of the shoulds and desperately want to unlearn them. Shoulds are the fucking worst!

You do you means doing what you want without worry-ing what other people will think. It's doing what's best for you and your happiness regardless of what others are doing around you.

Societal "shoulds" get in the way of what we actually need and want in life, but we also create some "shoulds" that are important for our well-being and success. The importance is understanding the difference between the two and recognizing the intentions behind your shoulds.

One way that we internalize the dreaded should is this idea about "living up to one's potential."

I HATE this idea.

"Your potential" has literally nothing to do with what you want or how you want to live, only what society deems "worthy" and "prestigious." If you're intelligent, you're supposed to be ambitious. If you're good at school, you're supposed to get an advanced degree and have a prestigious and successful career. "Your potential" is supposed to dictate your life based on how much everyone else thinks that you can achieve.

And it is garbage!

All these preconceived notions about what we need to achieve mean absolutely nothing if we're not happy. All these far-reaching goals are inconsequential if they're not actually something that you want to achieve.

We're constantly bombarded by the message that we need to have goals. We need to strive for success or we're stagnating, and then we'll never reach our potential. Nothing good comes from staying in your comfort zone. Those who have big dreams are those who change the world, after all, and don't you want to change the world?

Especially in a world where everyone has social media and we all have a limited view into the lives of others, it can be hard to keep from feeling like we're not doing enough. As they say, comparison is the thief of joy, and as I say, seeing all my successful friends on Facebook makes me feel like an utter failure as I sit on my couch watching reruns of *The Office* and gorging myself on parmesan Goldfish.

GOALS FOR THE SAKE OF GOALS

Like many other millennials, I had my life mapped out for me through the age of 22. Everything was planned for me through college. My goal in life was to graduate, and it didn't dawn on me how scary it would be to be directionless after that. I applied for jobs right out of college, but I had no idea which I would get and where I would end up. This lack of direction unsettled me. Once I got a job, I at least had some stability, but I had no other real goals than to wake up and get my ass to work every morning. It felt weird.

When I decided to go to graduate school, I felt much more comfortable. My need to have a goal and a direction was being fulfilled. I finally had a purpose again. When I decided that graduate school wasn't right for me, however, I had to adjust to being completely direction- and goalless again. And learning how to deal with that has been challenging.

After struggling with being without a goal or direction for some time, I realized that I am "goal-obsessed." This generally means that I set goals pertaining to *everything*. Big things, small things, inconsequential things, it doesn't really matter. I just feel more comfortable with a goal in mind. How many books I read, how much blog traffic I get, how much I eat. I think that goals can be a good thing, but being goal-obsessed has proven to be detrimental.

For me, being goal-obsessed means that I am constantly creating new goals for myself. I turn everything into a goal. Some of them are important goals that will affect my future, but for the most part, they're meaningless and arbitrary goals, the results of which will not affect my life in the slightest. I am even hesitant to incorporate new habits and activities into my regular routine, because completing them automatically becomes a goal, whether or not they will actually benefit me in any way. What's wrong with making arbitrary goals, you may ask? Nothing, unless you are plagued by crippling feelings of failure when you can't achieve a meaningless goal for yourself! See if you can guess who that is...

While I come up with the smallest goals for myself, I enter into a horrible phase of self-loathing when I don't complete them. On the other hand, completing a small, meaningless task leaves me with a lovely, fleeting moment of success.

So, you know, at least I'm balanced.

While this weird goal cycle is obviously unhealthy, it has also made me addicted to setting goals. This means that, as soon as I complete (or fail to complete) one goal, I immediately create the next one and start again. No "good job, Renata" or "you made it, Renata." Nope, just a proverbial kick in the ass to get moving on the next thing.

When setting goals like this, it becomes impossible to practice any mindfulness whatsoever. It's impossible to live in the moment when all that I can do is jump from one goal to the next without even a slight pause. This, unfortunately, doesn't create space for self-awareness either. When jumping from goal to goal without checking in on yourself mentally, it becomes challenging to understand yourself and your tendencies, your likes and dislikes. But who cares if you're happy and enjoying life if you're crushing your goals, amirite?

What I would really like to work on is celebrating the small victories. Any improvement should be reflected upon and celebrated. Any time that I take one small step towards a goal, or put my own mental health first, or do something new and scary. These all deserve to be celebrated, but they get overlooked when all I can do is create a new goal for myself. Not only this, but checking in to make sure that I'm happy with the result of achieving my goal. If I am not, maybe it's time for an about-face instead of blindly continuing down that path!

Once I realized how goal-obsessed I was and how arbitrary my goals could be, I did some classic Renata overcorrecting and decided to strive to set absolutely no goals. If the goals and results were meaningless anyway, what did it matter if the goals existed or not? I have been working on keeping myself from creating goals, but as you can imagine when your entire life has revolved around goals for 29 years, this is not the easiest thing to do. I've found that it helps to check how meaningful my goals are in order to decide whether or not I will hold myself to them. Sure, some goals are important, but when you create goals about *every little fucking thing*, some of them are bound to be absurd.

The most helpful thing that I have done on this journey, however, is to learn how to forgive myself. Failure is inevitable, especially if you have a bunch of tiny, insignificant goals that you have no control over. When the odds of failure are set that high and the stakes are obviously very low, it's important for me to learn how to forgive myself. Feeling disappointed in myself for every little thing is no way to live.

At this point, I haven't had much direction in my life for years, really. I'm finally getting comfortable with the fact that not every moment of my life needs to be planned out and that I'm not a failure if I miss the mark on some random goals that I create for myself. No need to create a plan or come up with some impossible thing to complete, I'm just working on finding what makes me happy and doing it, even if it doesn't mean that I'll achieve some impressive goal. I'm learning to be comfortable with just *being*.

The shoulds of goal setting and "living up to your potential" can make it impossible to feel settled and comfortable in this way. When you are constantly distracted by what you think you should be doing, it can be impossible to figure out what you actually like doing and to pursue it without feeling guilty.

"SHOULDS" AND GUILT

Shoulds manifest guilt. That is almost all that they do for us. They dictate our lives with imaginary boundaries that we must stay within or feel guilty for straying from. Have you ever heard someone use the term "guilty pleasure?" Maybe you've used that term before yourself. What if we didn't feel guilty about things that gave us pleasure? What if we read whatever books we wanted and watched whatever shows we wanted without shame and guilt? There's no reason for that guilt, after all. There's nothing wrong with watching reality TV or reading only YA romance novels. We just call them "guilty pleasures" because they're not what we're told we should like. Well, after years of forcing myself into the should boxes that I created, I realized that I was sick of feeling guilty.

You see, I've spent most of my life feeling guilty about, well, everything.

When relaxing, I feel guilty about not being productive. When I'm spending my free time being productive, I feel guilty for not relaxing. When I eat "bad" foods, I feel guilty, and then I feel guilty for feeling guilty. I feel guilty for spending money. I feel guilty for saying things I feel like I shouldn't have said, not saying things I feel like I should have said...the list goes on ad nauseum (and I mean that literally *since my anxiety makes me nauseous*).

As someone who feels perpetually guilty, one thing that I really appreciate is when someone else mentions one of their qualities (that I also have and feel guilty about because I don't think that I should have this quality) in a factual way. It really opened my eyes when one of my friends at college said that she was just more comfortable around women.

What? You mean I'm allowed to feel more comfortable around women without feeling ashamed? I don't have to feel as though I shouldn't be more comfortable around women? The way that she said it made it clear that she felt absolutely no shame about this quality. It was just a fact for her. "I feel more comfortable around women." *Shrug.*

Every time a friend makes a similar comment in passing, I notice again how guilty I feel on a regular basis for seemingly regular things. I think much of this is related to my afore-mentioned addiction to making goals – goals are meant to be achieved, and when they're not achieved, it is due to a lack of dedication, discipline, ambition, etc., and I should therefore feel ashamed. I see many tendencies that I have as a failure of some kind, one which clearly requires the penance of my constant and unnecessary guilt. Whether or not it makes sense, I attribute a positive or negative quality to all my thoughts and feelings...and usually, it is negative.

What it comes down to is that I have *a lot of feelings*, even about things that *don't deserve feelings*. Like I'm looking at the sentence I just wrote thinking, "Did I really need those italics? Should I hate myself for those italics?"

More and more frequently, as I face these feelings head-on, I'm realizing that the real issue is this need to classify every single thought that I have. For some reason, I've decided that every thought I have must be labeled as either positive or negative.

Wouldn't it be nice to not assign judgment to each thought and feeling? Wouldn't it be nice if thoughts and feelings could just...*be*?

Where have we heard this before?

As it turns out, this is actually one of the main pillars of meditation: allowing thoughts and feelings to come and go without attachment or judgment. Wanting to play a video game doesn't make me lazy or unambitious; it just means that I want to play a video game! Wanting to hang out with other people doesn't make me uncomfortable with myself or too needy, it just means that I want to socialize!

Then, of course, there's always guilt for past things, whether they were actually bad things that I did or just awkward moments that I replay in my head over and over. Having regrets is pretty pointless since we can't change the past, but we all remember cringeworthy things from our past just the same. When things like this come up, I like to remind myself that past Renata was just doing the best she could with the information she was given. She tried her best, and whether or not it was good enough doesn't really matter now, all that matters is the future.

I've really been able to start practicing this "no judgment" technique with my eating habits since working with my dietitian on "Intuitive Eating," which is literally just about listening to what your body wants and approaching food without judgment. Sweet foods are just sweet foods. Greasy foods are just greasy foods. Salty foods are just salty foods. None of these foods are "good" or "bad," they're just different types of food that your body can want at any particular time.

Since working with her, I've actually come to realize that my feelings of guilt around food are hurting me more physically and mentally than my eating habits ever have. Seriously, spending mental energy worrying about eating "good" vs "bad" foods always gives me an anxious stomachache, while listening to my body when it wants to eat fries and ice cream does not. Huh. It's almost like everything diet culture told us is a lie...

The practice of intuitive eating stresses that your body knows what it needs and that foods should not be labeled according to their relative "morality," so in order to correctly practice intuitive eating, you really have to learn how to eat without judging foods or yourself. Even now, trying to listen to my body and eat what I want, I judge myself for how well I'm doing. Am I listening to my body enough? The answer is almost always "no," which sends me into a guilt spiral.

However, the goal isn't to be perfect or to eat a certain thing; it's legitimately to approach food and myself without judgment. While I'm not there yet, putting this into practice with food has helped me to practice non-judgment in other areas of my life.

Back when I was practicing yoga regularly, I found my competitive nature often getting the better of me. When the yoga instructor would tell the class to come out of downward-facing dog whenever we were ready, I wasn't sure what they meant. I had always attributed my lack of stamina while working out to lack of willpower, so in my mind, I could probably hold a downward-facing dog for several hours if I kept my mind to it.

Obviously, this way of thinking was flawed for several reasons, not the least of which is that I wasn't listening to my body. Since I didn't trust my body's intuitive wisdom, I just "powered through" and tried to hold poses as long as possible. Once I started practicing intuitive eating and trusting that my body knew what was best, I started coming out of poses earlier without judging myself. I haven't perfected this, but just shifting perspective to listening without judgment is helpful. And then, hopefully, as I practice non-judgement more and more, it will continue to spread to other facets of my life.

I don't need to feel guilty about every little thing! I don't need shoulds controlling my life! Shoulds are not useful because they don't exist!

Instead of just living with this guilt and shoulds, I have decided to get to the heart of them. Why do I feel this way? Why does it matter? Then, I ask myself "so what?" So what if I do things differently than other people? So what if I don't reach that "potential" that everyone has decided I have? So what if I eat something that isn't quite "healthy?" SO. WHAT.

Want to take this approach, too? Grab a pen and go to the next page! It's worksheet time!

CHAPTER 2
WORKSHEET

We live our lives surrounded by "shoulds." Before we even start to form our own opinions on ourselves and the world around us, we're fed messaging on how we should feel. Whether this messaging comes from friends and family, authority figures, media, or the internet, there's always someone telling us how they believe we should feel.

And the worst part? WE BELIEVE THEM! Especially if this messaging is coming from multiple sources. Not anymore, I say!

Have you examined the "shoulds" that you're living with? Have you thought about those preconceived notions and why they're there? It's about time we evaluated those "shoulds" and decided which are serving us and which are not.

Below, there are three columns: "Should," "Why," and "So what?" For each preconceived notion that you have, I want you to write it in the "should" column. Next, in the "why" column, write why you feel that way. Is it for your own safety, wellbeing, or happiness? Is it from messaging you've heard your whole life? Is it from assholes on the internet? Finally, in the "so what?" column, write the consequence of this "should." Why is this "should" in place for you?

Check out the example below to guide you!

SHOULD	WHY	SO WHAT?
I should be in a higher-paying job by now.	Everyone else my age seems to have a higher-paying job than I do.	Having a lower-paying job will make others think that I'm a failure.

NEXT, here's where we get to the really fun part. If your "So what" has anything to do with anyone else like my example does, then I want you to "So what?" that again. So what if other people have opinions about your career? What does that mean for you? Continue to "so what?" until you get to the root of the problem.

Self-Compassion Time!

Is it just me, or do "shoulds" ruin everything?!

They give us unrealistic expectations of ourselves based on other people.

They force us into situations that we don't love solely because we're told those situations are how you become successful, happy, or (insert other personal goal here).

They make us feel ashamed for doing what's best for us when that's not the mainstream way to live.

But everyone is different! There are very few universal shoulds because everyone lives and feels differently. Plus, getting wrapped up in shoulds can keep us from living the lives we want to live. And life is too short to only focus on living up to others' expectations of us.

Accept that what you want is not always what everyone else thinks you should want. You cannot let shoulds define your career, relationships, or external appearance, but *especially* not who you are as a person.

CHAPTER 3

Cutting Through the Societal Bullshit Using Self-Awareness

HEN EVERYONE IN YOUR life (including you!) is comfortable with who you are, it can be tough when you want to make a change. You may feel like you shouldn't. But that's just shoulds getting in the way! Change is inevitable. Face any shifts to your self and identity with self-compassion. We need to be comfortable chasing what we want regardless of the should-based messaging around us and not feel bad when our wants and needs change.

WHAT'S WRONG WITH PHASES?

One of the pitfalls of extreme self-awareness that I've found is when I'm having a change in my identity. When you know yourself and self-awareness is one of your values, you can approach change almost indignantly. You were *so sure* of what you wanted, so that can't change now! You know who you are, every sparkling facet. So, when one of those facets changes, it can be very unsettling. There will probably even be some resistance, not related to the change itself, but to the fact that accepting that change would be accepting that you don't know yourself as well as you thought you did.

This is where phases come in.

Oh boy, one of my biggest peeves is how we have villainized and weaponized phases. We see phases used against other people all of the time, especially those in the LGBTQIA+ community.

"You'll understand when you're older."

"This will pass."

"You don't know who you are."

Phases have been used against us so much that we're afraid to change and afraid to admit we have changed. Going through different phases is seen as some sort of lapse in self-awareness on our parts. I'm sorry that I didn't know who I was going to be at the age of 50 when I was only twenty-fucking-five!

The thing is everyone goes through phases. Are you the same person you were 5 years ago? 10 years ago? Have your tastes in clothing changed since then? How about food? Relationships?

We all go through phases, but we've made people feel so ashamed for going through phases that we struggle to change and grow.

I had one coworker tell me about her sister who was in her late 30s. Her sister had always been interested in women but was suddenly feeling interested in men. My coworker fully supported her sister doing whatever (and whomever) she wanted, but she told me that her sister was still struggling. Everything that she had believed about her sexual identity was changing. I mean, after you hear phases weaponized against our LGBTQIA+ siblings for years, it's hard to not feel uncomfortable when something changes. She felt like she knew herself well enough and that this change would never come. She thought that she should know and understand her identity and that it would not change.

It's unfortunate that we feel ashamed about change when we change a lot throughout our lives. I still remember being asked in elementary school what I wanted to be when I grew up. *Elementary school.*

One day in my kindergarten class, our teachers handed out a paper that read, "When I grow up, I want to be ___." We were tasked with filling out the form and probably coloring it, or something. I don't quite remember this kindergarten exercise, but my parents have told me about it many times. On *Back to School Night*, when they came into my classroom and mine and my classmate's papers were displayed on the wall, amidst a bunch of pages that read "firefighter" and "astronaut," mine simply read "RICH."

What can I say? I was a girl who knew what I wanted.

This story always makes me think two things: first, 5-year-old Renata either thought that she would have enough energy to work every hour of every day through her 40s or that she was going to win the lottery somehow...you have to admire her optimism.

My other thought is: *HOW CAN THEY EXPECT A 5-YEAR-OLD TO KNOW WHAT THE HELL THEY'LL WANT TO BE WHEN THEY GET OLDER?!*

Of course, they didn't truly expect us kindergarten kids to know what we'd want to be when we grew up, but really, that's just how it begins. In high school, at the young age of 14, you're supposed to think about college and start planning where you'll go. Where you'll go to college is often related to what you'll study, so you need to know what you'll get a degree in when choosing a college. And that degree will hopefully get you a job in that field that you felt pressured to decide on before you were 18. So, you go to college studying something so intensely that you come out of the experience only knowing how to do what you studied, and then you get a job that pushes you further down the same-field rabbit hole.

So, recognizing this pattern, I repeat: *HOW CAN THEY EXPECT AN 18-YEAR-OLD TO KNOW WHAT THE HELL THEY'LL WANT TO BE WHEN THEY GET OLDER?!*

As unrealistic as it is that anyone will be able to decide on their profession at 18, that is the expectation. At every stage, we are tasked with knowing exactly what we'll want to do for a living as though it is final, when really, that is rarely the case.

We look back on our 5-year-old selves and laugh.

Ha! I wanted to be a vet? Little did I know that I hate schooling...and cats.

Wow, I thought that being a chef would be so cool, but I can't work under all that pressure!

I even laughed at my 5-year-old-self earlier in this chapter. We've decided that not knowing what we're going to do is somehow laughable and shameful. Twenty years later, we look back on our college years and laugh at our past selves. *Why did I think I'd be happy doing research? How could I not see sooner that that wasn't the right path for me?* (Okay, this one was actually me).

Now, every time I take on a new possible venture, I feel embarrassed. How can I not know what I should be doing by now? I applied, interviewed, and decided not to go to graduate school. I try a bunch of different side jobs every year. I applied to take more undergraduate courses. I got my life coach certification.

I have no idea what I want to do or be, ultimately. Am I a failure? Sometimes it feels that way. Plenty of people my age know where they're going, what they're meant to be doing. But even if several people know by my age what they want to do, it's okay that I'm still uncertain. There's nothing wrong with exploring and trying different things. Plus, who knows? What I want to do now may not be what I want to do in 20 years. With all of that pressure, beginning at, allow me to repeat myself, *five years old*, it's also hard not to get caught up in the overwork culture that exists.

OVERWORK CULTURE: KILLING US ALL SLOWLY

By the ripe, old age of 14, I had my first mental breakdown from being stressed out about schoolwork. My classmates and I were raised to believe that in order to get into a good college, grades weren't enough anymore. You needed to play at least one sport, be in at least three clubs, and volunteer for several hours per semester. Doing all these things became enviable because of the future that they supposedly guaranteed.

But what does it profit a stressed-out student to gain entrance into an excellent college, yet forfeit their soul?

In college, I pushed myself to overload on classes and work several jobs. I started suffering from depression in my late teens and anxiety in my early twenties. I was used to stress. I thrived in it. Plus, stress is what college is about, right? It's just *what you do*. You pull all-nighters and drink your fill of caffeine and eat french fries for at least three meals a week. That's how it's supposed to be, right?

Obviously, while this mindset is very unhealthy, it's also prevalent. One of the largest issues that I feel faces college students today is the immense amount of stress that is placed on them by the college and subsequently their peers. When I was in college, I called this phenomenon "The Busy Competition."

It seemed like every time I talked to someone around campus, as soon as I vented about one test or paper, I was suddenly in a competition that I had never planned to enter. The other person would give me a look that said, "oh, you think you have it bad," and then rattle off at least five assignments and two ways that their physical health was deteriorating from the stress.

I almost felt ashamed. Was I not doing enough? I had taken the time to sit down for a meal, to workout, to get a full night's sleep. Should I have sacrificed one (or more) of those in favor of my schoolwork?

It's almost as if your value is suddenly measured by how much you have to do, and how little sleep you've gotten. You must be shirking all your responsibilities as a student if you're also able to take care of yourself! This undoubtedly encourages an unhealthy lifestyle in college students. When you feel like you're always competing for who is busier, you start taking pride in how little you're able to take care of yourself. And that's messed up.

Doing all these things was necessary to get ahead, so when those excellent high school students (suffering from near-constant burnout) got into excellent colleges, they felt compelled to continue down that path. Trying to get into honors programs, taking on multiple jobs, taking extra courses to graduate early. Students are encouraged to fill all of their waking hours with extra-curriculars, and because of the added pressure, they feel as though time should come out of their personal care, not the time they set aside to study. After all, they worked so hard to get into this school. Can't screw it up now!

And it doesn't stop there. As they say, old habits die hard, and this overworking impulse doesn't stop after graduation. By the time we enter the workforce we are so conditioned to overworking ourselves that we start feeling bad only working 40 hours a week (you know, a *normal* workweek?). The system is set up in such a way that, since the few people who want to get ahead and make a lot of money need to overwork themselves, even the everyday worker is expected to kill themselves at work. No one should have to feel guilty about working a normal work-week and going home at 5pm on the dot, yet we still do.

Like any other student, I got swept up in this mindset my freshman year. I was pushing myself to my limits, and my health was suffering. I distinctly remember calling my mom on the phone one day and cry-yelling at her about something. Knowing me better than I knew myself in that moment, she asked me how much sleep I had been getting. I paused despite myself to think about what she was implying. You know, I really hadn't been getting much sleep lately...

My mom pointed out that I've always been sensitive to a lack of sleep, ever since I was a kid. In that moment, I started really considering my lifestyle. Did I want to walk around like a zombie and not have any balanced meals? Hell, halfway through my freshman year, I started getting headaches from being protein deficient.

I needed to make a change. I couldn't continue to abuse my body and assume that it would still work the way that I wanted it to. I started prioritizing myself again and working with my body's natural rhythms to get my work done. People were always surprised by how early I went to bed, but I knew that as long as I had a good night's sleep, I could tackle anything.

I promptly exited the Busy Competition, as well. I allowed anyone who wanted to compete with me to "win." But let's be honest, the Busy Competition has no real winners. The prize for the winner of the Busy Competition is a stress-induced heart attack by the age of 35. Great.

If someone wanted to out-busy me, they were welcome to. I didn't want my value to come from how busy I was. Did I still get pangs of doubt occasionally that I wasn't doing enough? Of course, I did. I actually still feel guilty whenever I am doing something that I don't deem "productive." I just remind myself that everyone needs breaks, and that my work will be even better for it if I allow myself a break every once in a while.

Things like sleep and meals are not optional. They're what we require to *live*. The next time you find yourself caught in a Busy Competition, just let the other person win. Honestly, the real prize here is *losing* the Busy Competition. The real prize is valuing yourself and your health, not how busy your schedule is.

While it might be nice to imagine a world where there is no external pressure to over-perform, I know that it's not the easiest thing to completely disregard. Exiting overwork culture and "The Busy Competition" becomes even harder when we start putting a positive spin on an overworked lifestyle and a negative spin on anything that doesn't follow the overworking culture narrative.

NOT THE COMFORT ZONE! ANYTHING BUT THE COMFORT ZONE!

As someone who strived to succeed from a young age, I was always looking for ways to improve and get ahead. Every leadership seminar, self-improvement book, and life coach that I talked to discussed the importance of getting out of your comfort zone in order to grow. You couldn't grow *and* be comfortable, after all. I heard the phrase "comfort zone" said as though it was a dirty phrase, only to be repeated in dark alleys by those who *aren't absolutely dedicated to growth.* And I certainly didn't want to be one of *those people.*

Similar to "the busy competition," I have had a tough time distinguishing how I feel about the idea of the "comfort zone" because of this mindset. I seemed to always surround myself with people who brag about their growth and how much they avoid staying in their comfort zone. While inside that bubble, it is easy to get swept up in feeling shame for wanting to stay in mine. If getting out of one's comfort zone was brag-worthy, shouldn't I be striving to do that as much as possible?

Also, like the busy competition, once I took a step back and reviewed this way of thinking, I realized how nonsensical it was. While those competing in the busy competition bragged about malnourishment and lack of sleep, those of us striving to avoid our comfort zones bragged about remaining uncomfortable for longer amounts of time.

Huh?

If you live life jumping from one uncomfortable thing to the next, you are literally setting yourself up for constant discomfort...and it took me a long time and much self-reflection to realize that I didn't want to live that way.

After a disastrous freshman year at college where I struggled to find where I fit in and ended up surrounded by people who made me feel less than for missing home, I decided to do something somewhat counterintuitive: come back to campus early for my sophomore year to help with freshman orientation. I was passionate about helping students like me who might struggle to integrate into college life, so joining the orientation staff initially had sounded like a no-brainer. However, as someone who literally had a meltdown every time I returned to campus after being home (through *senior year*, I might add), returning to campus early was not exactly appealing.

I remember the day that my parents brought me back to an almost-empty campus for my sophomore year so that I could begin orientation training. None of my roommates would be coming back until classes started, so my room was dark, quiet, and lonely. I asked my parents to stick around until I had showered and was ready to go to bed. My dad fell asleep on my bed in the main room, while my mom stood in the bathroom as I cried while I showered.

I knew that it hurt my parents to see me so upset, but sometimes you just need a good cry, you know? I did want to do orientation, and I think that orientation was worth the discomfort that I experienced. However, there was also an underlying shame to my tears.

Why couldn't I be like my other friends and feel fine returning to campus? I shouldn't be in tears about my parents leaving! I am such a baby!

Then, my mom said something that just clicked.

"Your dad and I live 20 minutes away from our parents...are we not adults? Your Uncle and his family live two doors down from his parents...is he not an adult?"

Obviously, my answer to these questions was no. In fact, when I first arrived at college and started talking with others, I was surprised to find that so many people's families lived so far away. Very few members of my extended family live farther than a half-hour drive away, so I struggled to imagine a world where the majority of my family wasn't close by.

It hadn't dawned on me that going 3 hours away to college would be difficult because I was always used to my family being nearby, which had made it even harder to accept that I was struggling.

Mom went on to ask, "Why would you do this to yourself? What's the point in making yourself uncomfortable?"

At first, the answer was easy. I couldn't just stay in my "comfort zone" (said with a scandalized voice) forever. Comfort was the root of all evil.

But...did that really make sense? If staying in your comfort zone is bad, and being comfortable should be avoided, does that just mean that I should live my life hopping from one discomfort to another and never feel comfortable? As someone who struggles with mental illness and general discomfort in my brain and body every day, the thought of that makes me shudder.

Up until then, I believed that discomfort was just something I was meant to "get over." This is probably one of the largest reasons that I've had trouble in the past recognizing the difference between dislike vs dread. I would do things that I *didn't even want to do* just to put another line on my resume. So, what if I hated it and was bad at it? It would make me (at least seem like) a better leader, right? Besides, if a little bit of discomfort leads to a bit of growth, shouldn't a lot of discomfort then lead to a lot of growth?

But alas, I found that there's a difference between doing something despite discomfort and doing something despite having absolutely 0% interest in doing said thing. There's also a difference between taking half of a step out of your comfort zone and taking giant leaps outside of your comfort zone.

Making yourself somewhat uncomfortable for the sake of growth is very different from compulsively avoiding comfort because you've been taught that being comfortable is a bad thing.

I would argue that you should always strive to do what makes you happy and helps you to be your authentic self. If that's hanging out in your comfort zone, great! If it involves taking a step out, go and get it! But stretching yourself way outside of your comfort zone just to do something that you don't want to do won't end well. It didn't for me, anyway.

So now, instead of automatically diving headfirst into something that will inevitably make me feel uncomfortable, I try to live in the moment and do what will make me happiest wherever I am. Sometimes, that means trying something new. Sometimes, that means hanging out on the couch and watching *Frozen 2* for the zillionth time. If what I'm facing is a once-in-a-lifetime opportunity, I will definitely take more time to analyze my feelings about it before I make a final decision. I try to figure out which path will lead to regret and do the opposite. The one thing that I am *not* doing is berating myself for craving comfort.

Whatever you choose to do day-by-day or moment-by-moment, just make sure that you're doing what is right for you. And don't feel guilty about chilling in your comfort zone, because choosing comfort isn't something to be ashamed of.

However, sometimes, growth and leaving your old comfort zone behind happens simply because you don't want to be in your comfort zone anymore. Sometimes, when we change, we simply start to outgrow our comfort zones. Like old TV shows we used to watch or old books we used to read, they just no longer appeal to us.

My first Halloween after I became a teenager, I remember asking my dad how I would know when it was time for me to stop trick-or-treating. I couldn't imagine a time would ever come when I wasn't interested in going anymore. My dad's birthday is on Halloween, so we've always had a big party, and up until then, going trick-or-treating with my cousins was part of the package. Obviously, adults don't trick-or-treat, so there had to be a Halloween when I would have to stop, but when would that be? Was there a universal age that people stopped wanting to go to their neighbors' doors for free candy? My dad gave me an answer that would always stay with me.

"This may sound crazy to you now, but the day will come when trick-or-treating just won't interest you anymore. The time will come when you just won't *want* to do it."

Of course, this did sound crazy to me, but recognizing that my dad probably knew more about growing up than I did, I just nodded. Lo and behold, sometime in high school, I just stopped feeling like trick-or-treating on Halloween. I mean, I even grew out of my favorite place on Earth, Chuck 'E' Cheese's. If I can outgrow that child casino, I can outgrow anything.

My comfort zone had simply changed. What I liked to do and what made me happy had evolved. What once had been a normal and comfortable tradition for me had to be cast aside for new and different comfortable traditions. I'm certain there are things and activities that everyone has outgrown from their childhood, and while it may seem like a silly example, to me, it is the most basic example of comfort zones changing.

Time and time again, I've seen that more often than having to force yourself outside of your comfort zone to grow, you *grow out of your comfort zone*. While many people argue that growth happens once you leave your comfort zone, I think this process starts long before.

It starts as an itch. An innocuous itch that something isn't quite right. At first you can ignore it, but as you grow and change, it becomes more apparent until it becomes more uncomfortable to live with it than to confront it. What once was believed to be your comfort zone has become *uncomfortable*.

Recently, I have been going through a sort of personal evolution. I've begun to feel uncomfortable in my current situation and have realized that I need to grow and change, even if only in small ways. It's almost as if I were a bug in a chrysalis, evolving and struggling against the barriers of who I was, knowing that bursting out is imminent.

I realized that what I had once considered my "comfort zone" actually wasn't at all comfortable anymore. Like a hermit crab in a shell that had gotten too small, I felt cramped in my comfort zone. It was almost time to crawl out and find a larger shell to inhabit. As my current comfort zone became less and less comfortable, I knew that it would be more comfortable, then, to move out of my old comfort zone.

Which made me realize that, oftentimes, leaving one's comfort zone isn't actually about being uncomfortable. It's about *seeking comfort*.

Read that again.

Growing into your authentic self takes courage, but I've found that the more you move towards being your authentic self, the less comfortable you feel in your past state of being. Bursting out of that smaller shell may seem scary at first, but as long as you're moving in the direction of living your own truth, you will feel more comfortable than you've ever felt!

A large piece of this puzzle for me, too, is that I find it far easier (and healthier mentally) to take gradual steps outside of my comfort zone as opposed to large leaps. A hermit crab doesn't move into a giant shell in one step, after all...it moves from shell to shell, each one incrementally larger than the last.

For me personally, taking those small steps helps me to expand my comfort zone. I realize that what I once thought was scary now isn't anymore! If I take a miniscule uncomfortable step towards who I want to be, I will probably end up more comfortable for it.

Large-scale steps, however, without the preparation of those smaller steps can set me up to crash and burn. Taking that unnecessary uncomfortable leap could cause me to feel as though the path I'm taking is incorrect, which can lead me to inevitably overcorrect in the other direction (as I am wont to do) and make me feel as though even taking small steps in that direction again would be fruitless. I also need to be in the right headspace to take on new challenges, which, according to Mas-Leo's hierarchy of needs, is a pretty specific (and fairly stable) headspace.

Think about your own hierarchy of needs. It was literally created to define in which states you can operate best and take on new challenges. You can use that to understand yourself better and decide how much you can handle at any given time. This is subject to change, of course, but it might help you better determine when you can take on extra challenges in your life.

Trying new things can obviously lead to discomfort, but staying in a situation where you are not true to yourself causes discomfort, too! While I don't think avoiding comfort is a bad thing, don't avoid the signs that you're growing out of your comfort zone either. Growth and change are inevitable, but they don't always mean jumping way outside of your comfort zone – don't fear change if it ends up making you *more* comfortable, that just means you're doing what's right for you.

It should be worth mentioning here that comfort seeking involves comparing long term and short-term health. For example, there are ways that we can seek short-term comfort that are unfortunately very harmful. Whether that be binging (literally or metaphorically) something detrimental to our mental or physical health or retreating to past, self-sabotaging ways, it is possible to have comfort mechanisms that are unhealthy in the long term, even if they feel comfortable in the short term.

Being comfortable is an inalienable right. There's no rule that says you need to live in discomfort.

It took me a very long time to unlearn this toxic idea that I must flee my comfort zone constantly to be successful. While that may work for some people, I just don't want to live my life in discomfort. Once I realized that I wanted to stray from this misconception, I was finally able to readjust my thinking and understand my own feelings about it, instead of blindly following what I had heard previously from teachers, life coaches, and peers. The fact of the matter is that self-awareness is not only knowing who we are and what defines us, but also discovering who we are not.

Do you think that the "comfort zone" isn't quite the villain that we make it out to be? Ready to seek out comfort instead of fleeing it?

Whether you love the idea of seeking comfort or are a bit wary of it, fill out the following worksheet and see if you can give yourself permission to seek comfort (at least occasionally!).

CHAPTER 3
WORKSHEET

Tons of people will have you believe that the "Comfort Zone" is something that should be avoided at all costs. Well, guess what? I want you to totally focus on your comfort right now. Instead of focusing on future ambitions and how you can grow and improve and yadda, yadda, yadda, I want you to think about those things that bring you the warm fuzzies. Maybe it's a special person, or a familiar place, or a certain book, or your favorite cup of tea!

Stop trying to push yourself out of your element just to see how much you can take! For this worksheet, I want you to focus on comfort. AND, if focusing on your own comfort makes you feel uncomfortable, sit with that for a bit. What is making you feel uncomfortable? How can you better appreciate yourself and what you need for comfort?

In the boxes below, write down every single thing you can think of that brings you comfort. Next, write down your "whys" (you had to know I was going to get to the "whys," right?). Why does this bring you comfort? What does this do for you? Finally, I want you to write down how you can apply this comfort to your everyday life and how you can find more of it to incorporate into your life. Check out my example below!

WHAT BRINGS COMFORT?	WHY?	HOW CAN I APPLY THIS TO MY REGULAR SCHEDULE?	HOW CAN I FIND MORE OF THIS?
My best friend	They're empathetic and understanding, so I always feel heard and loved	Schedule regular calls and visits with them that we add to our calendars	Seek other empathetic people and work on my own empathy so that I can feel heard and loved on my own

WHAT BRINGS COMFORT?	WHY?	HOW CAN I APPLY THIS TO MY REGULAR SCHEDULE?	HOW CAN I FIND MORE OF THIS?

Still having trouble? Think about times when you really needed comfort but didn't get it. What was the consequence of not getting the comfort you needed and deserve? How could you have made it different for yourself and made yourself at least *slightly* more comfortable? Add those ways to the sheet and see if they can help you the next time you're in a similar situation!

Self-Compassion Time!

We all need comfort every once in a while. When we were babies and wanted to be held, we screamed and cried until we were soothed. Now, give yourself permission to let that inner child out. You don't have to sob or throw a tantrum to get what you need — figure out what situations make you crave comfort and how you can bring that comfort into your life.

Are there any times in your life that you fled comfort because of the messaging that your comfort zone was bad? Imagine going back and approaching your past self and offering them the comfort they needed. Forgive yourself for not giving them that comfort and promise to give yourself more in the future.

Now, before you run off into the sunset and seek comfort, take a moment to look at your comfort seeking objectively: will this have a negative impact on me? And be realistic! Sometimes, we believe that something will have a negative impact because we are letting those darn shoulds get in the way. Will seeking comfort in this way cause you lasting mental and physical harm? Best to steer clear! Are you just hesitant about seeking comfort because you're choosing a different path than "the norm?" Go for it!

CHAPTER 4

Unlearning Who You Aren't and Becoming Who you Are

NOW THAT YOU'VE LEARNED these things, it's time to consider what other preconceived notions you're carrying that aren't serving you. Think about a time in your life where you allowed preconceived notions to dictate your decisions only to find out that you didn't agree with those preconceived notions at all! Which ideas have seeped into your subconscious and run your life?

It's time to reevaluate which ideas come from external sources and which come from within you. Let's unlearn some of the unhelpful stuff that doesn't define you!

BECOMING WHO YOU ARE

Much of becoming self-aware has to do with growing your own personality. Our personalities are influenced by others and outside forces far more than we realize. Especially as young people, our parents were huge influences on us.

At least for me, my parents were huge influences on who I was as a young person because they were my first friends. I watched the TV shows they watched, had dinner with them and their friends, listened to their music, went with them to the stores they shopped at, etc. When I went to college, I realized how much of what I liked was informed by what they liked. When left to my own devices, I did some of the same things they did, but also deviated a lot from my life with them. For example, I realized that if I were choosing which shows to watch, I would choose comedy sitcoms. My parents would far rather watch something with more depth and a more serious tone.

Much of becoming yourself is unlearning. Whether it's unlearning outside influences or unlearning how to be past versions of our own selves, this process is all about getting to the core of who you are and who you want to be while clearing out all of the noise. But we cannot do this unlearning without being self-aware. We can't do this unlearning without intimately understanding and questioning our patterns.

Even now in my late 20s, I am still unlearning what others have told me as truth. I was in a Facebook group recently, where an entrepreneur said that they were unapologetically chasing fame. "I want to be well-known, so what?" My immediate instinct was to feel that this person had poor priorities. They wanted to be famous? Really? Wow, they have a lot of work to do on themselves...

Then I reflected on what preconceived notion led me to that thought – I had wanted to be a household name as a young person, too, but when the influences around me told me that this was a silly desire, I cast it aside and assumed anyone who still had this desire to be naïve. Soon, they would understand their naïveté just like I had.

This is what preconceived notions do. They make us look down on others unnecessarily. *What's wrong with wanting to be well-known?* I wondered.

The only answer I could come up with was, "what's wrong is that they feel they can chase fame and I don't."

I was jealous. Jealous of their ability to unapologetically go after what they wanted. I was jealous that I had wasted so much time feeling guilty and squashing one of my desires while she felt comfortable talking about it flagrantly online.

It was a wake-up call for me. It forced me to take a hard look at my preconceived notions, where they came from, if they were actually what I believed, etc. Even something as simple as food had to be evaluated! What had I learned from others? What do I agree with? What do I disagree with? What needs to change?

TAKING OTHERS' ADVICE AND SEEING IF AND HOW IT CAN TRANSLATE TO YOUR LIFE

I realized that many of the things that I had been taught were not true, at least not for me. I was raised to believe that carbs were evil and to avoid the bread basket at restaurants at all costs, but I realized that I personally need carbs in my diet to stay full and the bread basket is one of my favorite parts of the meal. I realized that if I'm still hungry after dinner, it's not bad if I want dessert instead of more dinner. My body is not the same as everyone else's.

Part of the issue is that we want to believe that everything is one-size-fits-all. If that worked for my parents, it must work for me. But very few things in life are one-size-fits-all from jobs to hobbies to food to exercise to media consumption, the list goes on.

As we age, we learn what works best for us, and we learn that it's okay that we're not our parents or our peers or anyone else! We are able to pick and choose what we like and dislike as we grow into ourselves.

Like many young people, when I was a teenager, I struggled with my self-esteem. I spent much of my time in high school avoiding being vulnerable and staying out of the spotlight. My confidence had taken a sudden nosedive from the self-assured person I had been in middle school, and I felt the need to be a callous jerk in order to make up for that. As my mom watched my confidence level drop, she gave me one piece of advice:

"Fake it 'til you make it."

She said that few people have confidence in high school, so you just fake it until you have real confidence. For several years, I attempted faking confidence by creating distance between myself and others. I built a tough exterior and assumed that this lack of sensitivity meant that I was confident. This, along with various other influences that defined how to be popular and aloof, caused me to turn into someone that I didn't like or recognize. Trying to fake being a confident person only made me aloof and unhappy. I decided to adopt a new motto in protest: "Be true, be you." I think I even posted about it on Facebook back in 2011...along with every other update from my life every 2 hours.

Through college, I fully disavowed this notion of "faking it." I was trying to be a more honest and genuine person, and in order to fake anything, I was undoing the hard work that I put in to become myself. I wore my insecurities on my sleeve, and I tried connecting with people on a human level. I didn't want to hide my insecurities and snap at anyone who saw them anymore. I wanted to allow myself to build relationships based on respect and caring. Building relationships had always been the most important thing in my life, but now I was building them on honesty instead of fake confidence. That meant that my relationships could be deeper and more meaningful.

It wasn't until very recently that I realized that my mom's words didn't at all mean what I thought they did. "Fake it until you make it" never meant to pretend to be confident even when you have no confidence whatsoever in the hope that you'll magically gain some.

What it means is to let your true confidence shine through even when you're anxious. After fighting through the anxiety long enough, being confident will be second nature. I had thought that I needed to be dishonest when it came to being confident, but I don't. Being confident is all about knowing your strengths and understanding how to use them. Faking it until you make it is forcing yourself to exhibit that confidence that you have deep down, even when you'd rather run away and hide.

OWNING YOUR CONFIDENCE

I used to struggle with confidence particularly at my job. I found myself feeling incapable and getting defensive because of it. Now that I've accepted that I can be confident in what I'm doing, I'm relating to people much better, and I'm much more capable. I was always able to do my job well, but I let my own insecurities stand in my way. Instead of assuming that I don't know something and lashing out because of this lack of knowledge, I'm approaching problems with the thought that I probably do know the answer, and if I don't, then *that's okay*.

While I may be able to improve my confidence rather easily in some areas of my life, it can still be hard to be confident in myself when trying new things. When Josh and I started our podcast back in 2019, I was excited to start, but I was also nervous about how it would turn out. Most podcasts don't have long distance co-hosts like ours did. Would listeners feel that distance? Would we be able to come up with the time and energy to record every week? Would we run out of topics? Would listeners even find us interesting?!

When we started recording, I went from being somewhat unsure of myself to essentially being completely insecure. I adapted Mark Twain's saying, "it is better to remain silent and be thought a fool than to open one's mouth and remove all doubt." Although I talk very comfortably to Josh every day on the phone, I clammed up once we started recording. I felt like Rico from *Hannah Montana* when he tried to record a promotion for the surf shop, all happy and open, but then suddenly like a deer in headlights once the camera starts rolling. And if I tried to do anything scripted, it only got worse!

We were discussing topics that we had decided beforehand and that we liked. Why was I struggling so much? It wasn't until I started forcing myself to be confident that I really started enjoying recording. I had well-thought-out arguments. Why shouldn't I be loud and proud? It was then that I realized that I didn't have to *fake* confidence in order to *be* confident. I knew what I was talking about, I just had to own my confidence and make sure to speak up. The thought of being that vulnerable and making my opinions known was daunting. I would also have to put in much more effort to speak up and make my confidence known, but it was work that I knew I had to do in order to make our podcast better. Plus, learning how to be more confident in myself would help me be more capable in other areas of my life and be more honest with myself and others. There's no downside!

I would never give anyone the advice that they should be fake. But owning your confidence doesn't make you fake. In fact, it can only make you more genuine. Recognizing what you know and what you're capable of is just another way to get to know yourself better and be your genuine self. Plus, confidence feels much better than insecurity. Who wouldn't want to be more confident?

Think about talents and skills you know that you have. Now, imagine claiming those talents and vocalizing them to someone else. How does that make you feel and why does it make you feel that way? What would it take for you to be able to confidently and comfortably own your talents?

Dig down deep, find your strength, and force it out if you need to. Unapologetically own your confidence. As long as you're being true to who you are, it'll get easier.

Okay, so I don't know that for sure, but I'm hoping that it will. For the both of us.

But before you can be true to who you are, you need to know exactly what you're about...

HONING IN ON WHO YOU ARE AND WHO YOU AREN'T

Last summer, while attending one of my yoga studio's classes in the park, I was prompted to set an intention for my yoga practice, and I decided on "living my truth."

For anyone who doesn't know what a yoga intention is, it's essentially what you want to focus or meditate on during class. I've heard instructors call it "the reason you stepped onto your mat." Did you come to your mat looking for tranquility? Balance? Peace? Movement? No matter what it is, that's your intention for your practice.

I was in a moment where I felt like a big life transition was coming. I had been working from home for several months, I was getting my coaching certification, and I was trying to figure out what I wanted to do with my life. I needed some guidance. What could be better than asking the universe for guidance that aligned with who I was, and even more importantly, who I was becoming?

I had a poignant moment weeks later when I started talking to a startup company that I would eventually work for — I realized that working for them would be living my truth. Small, hip startup, out of the corporate world, where I would be creating content and marketing materials as well as countless other things, this just aligned perfectly with who I am as a person.

Since then, I've almost taken on this idea of "living my truth" as my creed. When making difficult decisions, big or small, I sit back and ask myself, "Does this align with my truth? Will this help me be more myself/more of who I'm becoming?"

It may sound cheesy, but honestly, decision-making this way has become super valuable for me as someone who prides herself on self-awareness. As you've already read, we often outgrow our comfort zones as we grow into who we're becoming and things that go against our core values can make us uncomfortable. So now, if something's making me uncomfortable, I try to see if that's because I'm moving away from myself and my beliefs.

Graduate school wasn't for me because being super enthusiastic is who I am, and I wasn't entirely enthusiastic about graduate school. Graduate school in general was going to be more work and sacrifice than I wanted to do and more than would be normal for me, but also being unenthusiastic was a red flag. Recognizing that something isn't on-brand for me has helped me to come closer to living my truth.

That being said, I think that this way of thinking can easily trap us if we don't allow ourselves the ability to grow and change if we're so caught up on who we are right now. Several years ago, I remember going out shopping and seeing something in a clothing store that I liked. I don't remember what it was, but I thought "damn, I wish I was the type of person who wore this."

How foolish! There's nothing barring me from wearing anything but myself. As someone privileged enough to be able to fit into clothing from most stores, I could wear whatever I wanted, no matter what my "style" or my "brand" dictated. I could wear whatever and change my brand up at any time. Just because I had never worn that article of clothing before, doesn't mean that I never could! Or just because I didn't enjoy the experience of wearing that article of clothing before, doesn't mean that I wouldn't like it now!

YOU define your brand, which means who you are can change at any time. Only you decide who you're going to be and how to move closer to living your truth.

The one caveat to all of this is to not get stuck on superlatives! Identifying yourself as anything with relation to other people can be a dangerous game because no one is the same and people are always changing. If you pride yourself on being the prettiest person or the most intelligent person or the loudest person or the most interesting person in the room, you may be in for a rude awakening when you meet someone prettier, smarter, louder, and more interesting than you. You can define yourself any way that you like, but using superlatives can lead to feeling resentful of others and like you are not good enough. You can identify as any of those things without identifying by their superlatives (and then suffering the subsequent identity crisis when someone surpasses you). Just don't get hung up on those superlatives!

If you're like me and overthink every decision in your life (primarily because you feel like every decision must follow a pattern and mean something even if it really doesn't), trying to weigh your decisions against who you are and your truth can be a helpful tool, not only to help you move in the direction of who you want to be, but also to help you change things about yourself that don't align with that.

CHANGING WHAT YOU DON'T LIKE ABOUT YOURSELF

When I was in college, I attended a leadership conference where we chose personality traits that were important to us, whether it was having this trait ourselves or seeking out others with these traits. Many of the other people in my group were surprised to see that while "compassionate" and "empathetic" were two traits that most of the other people had on their lists, they were absent on mine.

Empathy and compassion were just two traits that I didn't really have in my relationships previously. We mostly just bonded on shared sarcasm and enjoyed the same TV shows. Empathy and compassion were never traits that even crossed my "good personality traits" radar.

But of course, the point of college is to meet all different kinds of people. College is where I met so many awesomely empathetic people, and I knew that I wanted to be like them. So, I set out on my journey to become more empathetic.

Up until that point in my life, I had been functioning with the smallest amount of empathy possible. I wasn't great at relating to others and was quick to anger when someone felt an emotion that I didn't really understand. After interacting with my newly found empathetic friends for a few months, I realized that I wanted to become more like them. I wanted to be able to have deeper connections with people who were not only based on mutual interests, but also on the emotions and quirks that made us different. It's been a few years since I started practicing empathy, and, while I will never fully become an empath, I'm proud of the strides I've made.

My first step in becoming empathetic was to become aware of my own emotions and how I respond to the world around me. This was a fun part of the process for me because I actually enjoy learning new things about myself. I love learning how my mind works and what makes me tick. As ever present as my self-hatred can be, it has never stopped me from digging deeper into my brain.

The side-effect of all of this self-exploration is that I started on an endless loop of self-assessment. I now struggle to actually live in the moment because I'm constantly checking in to see how I feel. Which can be awesome and insightful, but also really irritating. Who knew that focusing on how you feel could have such long-lasting effects?

With the knowledge that I gathered with this newfound self-awareness, I was able to decide how certain words or situations made me feel based on my own experiences. This emotional exploration for me was very different from previous self-exploration I had done. I am a tried-and-true "thinker," who relies on thoughts far more than emotions. More than one therapist in my life has called me out for answering the standard therapy question "how do you feel?" with my thoughts instead of my emotions.

Exploring my emotions was entirely new for me, but necessary in order to not only become empathetic, but to begin to face any emotions that I had been repressing. As I allowed myself to experience and understand my feelings, I found myself becoming a bit softer and more sensitive. Now, instead of completely ignoring any negative feelings, I accepted and explored them. Why did I feel that way and how could I heal myself? Instead of berating myself for negative feelings, I treated myself with more compassion. I learned what emotional triggers I had, and I stopped feeling wrong for having them. In the end, I became a kinder person because I stopped saying or doing things to others that would have hurt me.

I truly believe that none of this self-improvement would have been possible without therapy. I started going to therapy for my depression, but it also helped me become a kinder person by enabling me to become more sensitive. From the safety and comfort of my therapist's couch, I was able to crack my own tough exterior and allow myself to be more vulnerable. Recognizing my vulnerabilities, and that I didn't want them to be attacked, made me want to actively try to not attack others' vulnerabilities. Being honest about my own emotions meant that I could allow others to be honest about theirs.

Once I took stock of my own emotions and started being a bit kinder, the next step was infinitely more difficult: accepting others' emotions even if I didn't understand them.

First, I would need to recognize that others have different triggers than I do. I changed my strategy from only avoiding saying things that would have hurt me to learning how to word my thoughts in a sensitive way to avoid hurting anyone else.

I knew the topics that my loved ones found triggering, and I began speaking as carefully around them as I possibly could. I paid attention to how I worded certain things and how my words could be perceived by others. It was important for me to understand that, despite my best intentions, I could still hurt others with my words, and I wanted to avoid that at all costs. While I can't be held responsible absolutely for the way that others feel, I can at least understand that we are not the same person, and I can be mindful of their emotions despite our differences.

The last, and most important, part of this journey has to be acceptance: giving others a space to be honest about their emotions and being tolerant of those emotions. I've begun letting others know that I am happy to support them in any way that I can, while recognizing that the type of support they need may not necessarily be the type of support that I would have needed. I just allow others to be themselves and accept them as they are.

This empathy has helped me to have deeper relationships, especially with myself, and allowed me to make changes to myself and my personality that better aligned with who I wanted to be.

And one of the large ways that I have changed my life is becoming unwaveringly honest.

EVERYONE DESERVES TO CHANGE

You know what they say: "people never change."

I'm not totally sure that I agree with that.

Don't get me wrong, I don't think that the ex who you broke up with 2 months ago who is swearing that they've suddenly grown up has actually changed, but if people want to change and grow, they do!

Just think about it — are *you* the same person that you were 5 years ago? 10 years ago?

If you're anything like me, your response to that will be something like "No, and thank goodness for that!"

We all grow and change. Our looks change, our relationships change, our interests change, and even our personalities change. Every new experience we have, person we meet, life change we experience, they all inform the person that we become, for better or for worse.

Becoming a fully mature adult who handles others' emotions and confrontation well takes time. The vast majority of us don't come anywhere close to being able to manage this until our 20s or 30s. Hell, some people struggle with it their entire lives.

I've mentioned a bit about my high school personality and about how guarded and vulnerable I was as I entered my teen years. To be honest, one of the most pivotal parts of my teen years was when I realized how much of a jerk I was. Sure, I was proud and unwilling to be vulnerable, but unfortunately, I was also dishonest.

Because I was callous, I told myself and others that I was just "brutally honest," happy to put anyone down when I deemed it necessary, but in reality, I was only selectively honest. I lied by omission for my own selfish reasons, stringing people in my life along in different ways. I made excuses for myself, but once I graduated high school and started really working on who I was becoming, I realized that I couldn't face myself anymore. For someone who was "brutally honest" I sure as hell wasn't honest with these people. I apologized to the people that I wronged, but I knew that an apology wasn't enough until I actually did something about it.

So, I started working on being more honest. I turned on my "read receipts" so that anyone who texted me could see if I read their messages. I started telling people how I really felt and being forthcoming with my thoughts, even if they weren't pleasant for others to hear. Unfortunately, being 100% honest all the time can make someone be somewhat tactless. Because of this, this personal work really had to go hand and hand with becoming an empathetic person. I not only wanted to be honest with those around me, but I also wanted to understand when it was appropriate to share. I worked on understanding that my truth isn't everyone's truth, and that's okay. If someone asked me how they looked in a new shirt, I learned that instead of automatically saying, "Oh *I feel* like it's too tight/too loose/too blue/too short/too long..." I would ask, "How do you think it looks?" or "How do you feel in it?" Beauty is in the eye of the beholder, and my eye is not nearly as important as the eye of the person in the shirt and how they feel!

Now, the word "dishonesty" leaves a bad taste in my mouth. In typical Renata fashion, I have completely overcorrected. I strive to be as honest as possible at all times. This sounds great in theory, however, talking to me can be a complete nightmare. Because of this compulsive honesty, I tend to overshare because I want my interlocutor to understand the story from every angle. No story that I tell is straightforward and easy. You need to understand the backstory, and I mean *every bit of backstory*, which can make even the simplest of stories lengthy. "You see, I was born 5 pounds and 6 ounces on the morning of February 24th..."

I also strive to make sure that I am as clear as possible so that I cannot be called out as a liar on a later date. In order to do this, I obviously have to think about what I'm saying from every possible angle and the different situations in which that particular fact could come up. It's a good thing that I was an overthinker already, because there's no way I wouldn't have become one with this approach!

I went from having no filter by way of being "brutally honest" to having no filter because I just tell everyone *everything*.

I am constantly going out of my way to overshare and be fully transparent. I am all about relationships, and I want to know who I am going to get along with right off the bat. What does that mean? Oversharing and giving way too much information and insight into my life so that we can see if we vibe, of course! How can you be close to someone if they don't thoroughly understand your childhood trauma? You can't!

Of course, this classic Renata overcorrecting comes with some backpedaling. I've learned that not everyone wants to hear every intimate detail of my life. I've begun to understand that not everyone is mentally prepared to hear about my mental health issues at any moment. Honesty is great, but overwhelming everyone and non-consensually oversharing constantly is not. I can be honest and make those around me comfortable, but it's taken me some time to find the right balance.

Being vulnerable about who you are and what you stand for is not always easy. We all struggle with it from time to time, but there is power in being vulnerable with others, especially those you love and respect. One of the keys to being vulnerable is recognizing when you need help and being courageous enough to reach out for it.

BEING VULNERABLE AND ASKING FOR HELP

I have no idea where I got the idea that asking for help was indicative of weakness and incompetence, but for some reason, that's what I believed for a long time. I've always been an overachiever for seemingly no reason, but it seems as though my imposter syndrome has convinced me that I not only need to do everything, but that I need to do everything alone or else I'm worthless. Obviously, this isn't true, but it can be hard to remember we can ask for help, especially if we have the idea in our heads that there are certain things we shouldn't need help with. Life isn't a competition of who needs less help, though! It's important to make your needs known.

My first job is where I started learning how to ask for help. After having been overloaded with work to the point of snapping mentally and neglecting some of my work, my manager started getting concerned. She explained I needed to ask for help before it got to the point where we were practically losing business. Once I got over the idea that asking for help implied incompetence, I was able to step back and realize that asking for and receiving help would actually be better for the company than having me try to do everything. I would be doing my manager a favor by asking for help. Who'd have thought?

This desire for help comes with a certain amount of communication and honesty, not just with yourself, but also with others. After all, no one can know if you need help, or help you, if you don't ask. Not only do you need to be able to communicate that you need help, but more importantly, you need to be able to articulate what you need. As I learn to be more open about asking for help, I become more open about all kinds of discomfort. If I am going into a doctor's appointment for a procedure, I explain to them exactly which parts of the procedure I don't like so that they can proceed with caution and often talk me through it. Every person who has had to give me a needle within the past few years knows I am afraid of needles and makes every effort to make me as comfortable as possible. Even if making me comfortable isn't in their job description, most are happy to help me as opposed to having me squirm or cry on their exam table.

But don't overlook the fact that you can even ask your friends and family for help in your everyday life. So many people out there want to help you if you give them a chance. I especially endorse asking your parents/family/mentors for help sometimes. Sure, you want to make it in the world on your own and figure things out by yourself, but relying on those with a vested interest in your success could be beneficial not only for you, but for them too! People (parents especially) like to feel needed. Sometimes asking them for help and allowing them to feel needed is actually helping them as well.

So, give your mom a call and ask about that recipe. Reach out to a connection who specializes in one of your passions. Let your friends know when you need them. The people who love you want to help you – give them that opportunity. Just don't forget to make sure they know they can turn to you for help, too!

Sometimes, it's challenging admitting that we need help and being vulnerable with ourselves. This starts with knowing who we are, what we stand for, and most importantly, *why*. Want to get real about what makes you who you are? You guessed it! It's time for a worksheet!

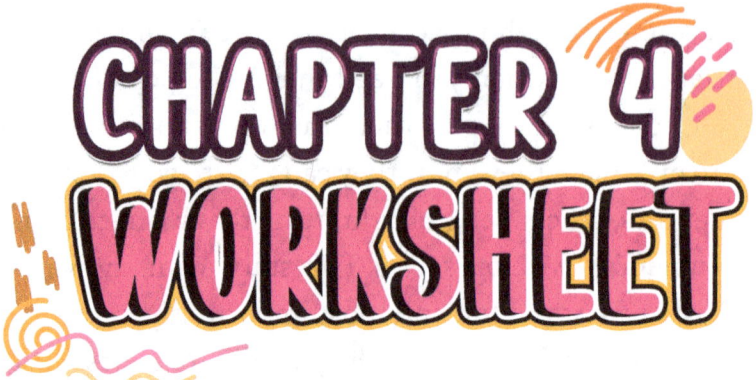

CHAPTER 4
WORKSHEET

When it comes to "living your truth," it's important to do so both outwardly and inwardly. Living an authentic life is what makes us feel the most comfortable in our own skin. If we're living for others, we're not living our own lives at all, just a life that someone else wanted for us — and that's no way to live!

I want you to think of the best "personality picture" you've ever taken. Seriously, that first image that came to mind when you read "personality picture." It doesn't matter if it's wacky or serious or taken with your favorite people or in your favorite place. Maybe it's an image of you accepting an awesome award! Whatever that image may be, I want you to print it and paste it into the box below that says "My Personality Picture." In the box across from that, I want you to write what it is about your picture that makes it a personality picture for you.

MY PERSONALITY PICTURE

DESCRIPTION

This picture was taken after a terrible breakup, so it reminds me how resilient I am. The red hair and weird face remind me that I'm a quirky and fun individual. I'm also wearing a quarter zip sweatshirt, a shoutout to my preference for comfort, especially in my day-to-day wardrobe.*

*You can see my personality pic in all of its glory in the appendix!

Next, write down things that you love and make you feel good *inwardly*. Is it mentoring younger people? Painting? Doing escape rooms? Traveling? Learning? When do you feel most alive and most yourself? Write. It. Down.

Next, it's time to get to your "whys." Ooooh! I love this part! You currently have a list of "whats."

This activity brings me joy! My grandma's necklace is my favorite piece of jewelry! I love this song and the happy memories that come with it!

That's great, but "whats" only get you so far. After all, that activity you *love* might not spark as much joy in a different context, someone else's grandma's necklace might not hold nearly as much meaning for you, and that song might not resonate with you nearly as much without the memories behind it. Dissect each and every one of your "whats" and figure out why they help to define you.

These "whys" are what will help you live your truth. Time and time again, when faced with a decision in life, make sure to come back to your "whys" to help you move in a way that will make you feel like you are living in authenticity. Seek out more of your "whys" to increase joy in your life. Just remember not to overload yourself! Make sure to make enough time for all your "whys" – productive and relaxing alike!

WHAT ARE MY WHYS?

Helping people feel less alone and less ashamed to be who they are

*Remember that nothing is set in stone here! Your "whys" might change throughout your life. They might not. Give yourself permission to grow and change.

Finally, I want you to imagine your ideal self and who you want to be. Think about both your insides and outsides. What does this "ideal you" look like? In the boxes below, write all about this future you. Do you want to dye your hair a million colors? Be an international trendsetter? Or even just learn to be someone who can *relax* without feeling guilty (yes, this one's me!)? Hell, maybe you're cool just being you – I love that! How can you be even more YOU?

Then, for each quality you wrote for your ideal self, write the FIRST STEP to getting there. Just the first! Let's not get overwhelmed here!

IDEAL ME ON THE INSIDE

Confident, empathetic, giving myself grace when necessary, comfortable in my own skin.

IDEAL ME ON THE OUTSIDE

Probably tattoos, but of what? Comfortable (but also sexy and badass) clothing. Writing regularly and in a job I'm passionate about.

FIRST STEPS...

- *Work with my therapist on confidently asserting boundaries and learning to forgive myself.*
- *Only buy clothes that suit my personality.*
- *Make time to write every day.*

Self-Compassion Time!

Thinking about who your "ideal you" is can give you clarity when making huge life decisions like your career, where you live, your relationship configurations, etc. Try to keep your "ideal you" in mind when you make any and every decision, even the smallest ones. Seriously, try to think of your reasoning behind every decision you make and see if you're focused on your higher self. If not, maybe it's time to reassess and see how you can better live your truth.

Living your truth is the way to live a fulfilled life. After all, didn't you feel most alive and happy when you were being the most yourself? We all feel good when we're being the truest version of ourselves and living in accordance with our "whys."

Care about yourself enough to follow your bliss and live your truth. Care about yourself enough to build your ENTIRE DAMN LIFE around your "whys" and who you want to become.

You deserve it.

CHAPTER 5

Letting Your "Whys" Guide the Way

NOW THAT YOU KNOW your "whys," it's time to build your life around them. So easy, right? All done and we can stop now? You've got it from here. As much as I believe you do have it, we still have one more chapter and worksheet to go.

IDENTIFYING YOUR "WHYS"

It can be challenging to embrace your "whys" when the world around you thinks that you should have different whys. Maybe you didn't even realize that having other "whys" was an option until *right now*.

But people having all different "whys" is what makes the world go 'round! As my great-grandmother used to say, "that's why they make chocolate and vanilla." So, I have decided, with the power vested in me, by self-publishing platforms everywhere, that you should passionately and uninhibitedly chase the life that you want.

For me, once I realized my "whys," so many doors opened for me.

I realized a while ago that people are my passion. Not necessarily some large-scale altruistic desire to make the world a better place, but more or less loyalty and human connection. I am always happy to move my schedule around just to be with others and get to know them better. Relationships are worth prioritizing.

This is how I've always felt, too. As a child, I lived for deep, late-night conversations at sleepovers, I loved finding new things that I had in common with my peers, and I only participated in after-school clubs because I could interact with my friends in different environments.

My opinion on every experience I've had in my life is based on the relationships that I've made. If you ask me how I felt about any particular competition, retreat, or event that I've attended in my life, I'll talk you ear off about the people that I met and what we did. As difficult as my college experience was, I look back knowing that I wouldn't change it for anything because of the people I met and how they shaped me.

One of the most intoxicating feelings that I've ever had in my life is the sense of belonging to a group. There's just something about that feeling when you're with people who totally *get* you, your jokes are landing, and you're all laughing together. I've known that I love that feeling ever since I was a scared kid going from my middle school friends, who I knew so well, to an all-new set of high school students. That sense of belonging is rare, but it's one of the best feelings in the world.

I try to relate everything in my life to others. If you were to tell me that you like a particular song, food, or color, then, every time I saw or thought about that particular thing, I would think "Oh, this is that song/food/color that (insert name here) likes!"

When I am telling someone a story (one of the 10 people in my life that I literally tell everything to), I find myself frequently relating what I am saying to this particular person to what I've said several times before when telling the story. "It's like I was telling Dan, Marisa, Josh, Julia, my mom, my hairstylist, my therapist, the mailman, and the cashier at Wawa today..." I've definitely heard other people do this, but nowhere near as much as I do. I've been trying to cut back on this habit for the sake of the person I am talking to and trying to get to the point in a quicker, less-convoluted way, but, when your brain is connecting every damn story and every fucking feeling to another person (and you've decided to completely remove whatever verbal filter you've ever had), it's tough!

Almost all of my personal goals involve people in one way or another. When it comes to my writing, it's all about making people laugh and creating content that others can relate to. When I'm conversing with my friends, I am constantly trying to create a platform that makes them comfortable sharing things with me. Sometimes this involves majorly oversharing, but so be it! If I have to make you feel uncomfortable in order to make you comfortable, then that is what I shall do! I never said I was perfect...

This is probably why I enjoyed dating so much. It was great to have an excuse to overshare with someone like crazy in order to see if we were compatible. Learning about people is really the best, especially when I can send them home after and only talk to them when I want to!

I even took this a step further when I was dating and decided to also practice polyamory. As someone who has a huge passion for people (and completely rejects the mainstream notion that your paramour should always be the primary person in life over friends and family), I decided that I wanted to be able to date multiple different people without putting one particular paramour above any other. I've always held strong love for multiple friends at once, so this suited me perfectly – I was able to express the love I held for multiple people while also keeping my friends at the same level as my love interests. It was a win-win. It was great to have a way to build my romantic life around my main passion: people.

When I was on a leadership retreat in college, we all had to give someone in our group a compliment, and my sorority sister had said that I made her feel like she could be herself around me without judgment. She could not have given me a better compliment. But I knew that I could still do better. My personal project for the last several years has been to become an empathetic person so that I can make others feel like they can be themselves around me. As a typical "Thinker" on the Myers-Briggs scale, it's been an interesting exercise.

My life coach asked me recently when I felt the most satisfied and fulfilled. I thought back to all of the things that I had been proud of in my life (projects at work, motivational speeches, and obstacles I've faced), and I couldn't say that I had ever felt truly fulfilled. Like Angelica Schuyler, was I cursed to never be satisfied?!

But once I expanded my scope a bit and thought about my life as a whole – and not just my accomplishments – I realized that having personal, 1-on-1 conversations about others' feelings and opinions is very satisfying for me. This is the space where true bonds are formed. Whether we agree or disagree, this is where I can see people come to life – I see their faces light up and their hands gesticulate wildly.

This is where I live.

And those true bonds aren't formed overnight nor are they formed talking about the weather. I want those deep talks. I want to talk about traumas, mental illnesses, kinks...I want to hear what makes the other person who they are and what makes them feel insecure. As you can imagine, this makes me really fun at parties...

This means that I primarily connect with others that actually want to engage with me about these topics. This "why" for me means that I don't waste my time (or the other person's time!) trying to become close with people that only enjoy having surface-level friendships. We'll never work, so let's leave it at that. Channeling your "whys" and being yourself right off the bat can save you from all types of relationships that would be totally wrong for you. Be yourself, and attract other people who will light you up and enrich your life.

Recently, I was sitting with my cousin as she lamented making the decision of whether she should transfer into our local 4-year college either as a freshman or sophomore. While she wanted to stay at community college and save money for as long as possible, she was understandably worried about starting at the new school as a sophomore after everyone had already made friends. So, I gave her the advice that I've used that has started (and probably also ended) many potential friendships.

"When you're with a bunch of people, overshare *just a little bit* and see how everyone reacts. Those who nod along in agreement are your people. Those who look at you slightly worried and inch away from you are probably not people you wanted to get to know anyway!"

She immediately got a first-hand glimpse of this method in action when her mother walked into the room and complained about how cold it was. I replied with an off-hand comment about the effects of the cold weather when (like me) you've decided that bras are no longer for you. I couldn't help but smile when my cousin excitedly pointed out that I had just demonstrated my lesson. The kid is a quick study.

Unapologetic oversharing has led me to both the most awkward moments of my life as well as the most authentic. And let's be honest, wouldn't you rather be true to yourself than to pretend to be someone you're not forever? Self-acceptance is such an important step to living authentically.

As you might be able to tell from this book, self-acceptance is another one of my "whys." Of course, this also relates to my passion for people because I want to help others accept themselves, too. I know, you're entirely shocked. That's not what this entire book was about or anything!

For me, one of the hardest parts of self-acceptance has been accepting my body. With patterns of disordered eating haunting me throughout my life, it has been challenging for me to accept and love my body the way that it is. When I was younger, I was willingly at war with my body. Starving myself, shaming myself for eating, and over-exercising were regular activities for me.

As I got older and accepted that my relationships with food and my body were dysfunctional, I realized that in order to fully take care of myself, I couldn't only accept and love all of my thoughts and feelings in my mental world, but I also had to accept and love my physical self, too. My dietitian (and amazing book beta reader!) Kelsey introduced me to the concepts of "intuitive eating" and "intuitive movement," two concepts rooted wholly in self-acceptance. These practices are exactly how they sound – eating and moving intuitively with whatever my body is calling for in the moment. As someone who practices yoga, I was all too familiar with hearing a yoga instructor tell me to do whatever my body called for, but apparently, this intuition doesn't only stop when it comes to taking a child's pose when you need it!

In order to embrace intuitive eating and intuitive movement, I had to learn to trust my body and accept it the way that it is. Since these practices completely reject the idea of having an "ideal weight" and trying to lose weight, practitioners must accept their bodies for how they are. For example, my body craves French fries regularly. While my past self may have constantly berated myself for craving French fries and forced down some salad instead, I'm working on accepting these cravings and giving my body what it wants. Can you be healthy and eat intuitively? Of course. But I don't always want to eat healthy. And I've decided to accept my body and this choice. It's okay body, let's get you some French fries!

Self-acceptance has been (and will continue to be) an important part of my journey and a passion that will inform the way that I live my life from all facets: personal, social, professional, etc. One of the ways that I express this passion is through yet another one of my passions: writing.

USING YOUR "WHYS" TO INFORM YOUR DECISIONS AND GOALS

I have always been a writer. From writing poems and random stories as a child to writing this book, writing has always been something that I've turned to when I feel like creating something. As a wordsmith, creating pieces of writing gives me a sense of purpose. There's really nothing like putting pen to paper (or, more typically today, putting fingertips to keyboard) and creating something awesome. I have not written consistently throughout my life, but whenever I have had any really creative ideas, they have become writing projects (or at least pieces of writing projects). As someone who works in small bursts of energy and is easily bored, many of my writing projects are single chapters, scenes, or sentences that never become anything. But the promise of a great idea is still there, and even that feels good.

When I was in elementary school, I was inspired by writers like Dr. Seuss and Shel Silverstein. I wrote journal after journal full of poetry. Some of it was silly, but some of it was deep (well, as deep as a nine-year-old can be). When I was in 4th grade, my entire elementary/middle school competed in a poetry contest. A group of local poets graded our poems against each other and gave the top three poets of each grade a plaque.

I still remember how it felt sitting in the pew of our school's chapel with my heart racing, waiting to hear the results. As someone who wrote books and books of poetry for myself, I felt like this was the moment that would truly define whether or not I was a good poet. I completely lost the wind from my sails when they announced that they were going to group and rank grades 4th-8th together – how was my 4th grade poem supposed to compete with the poems of the middle school-ers?! – and even more dismayed when my name wasn't called when they announced the first, second, third, and honorable mention for our classes.

That is, until they announced the grand champion, the top poem in the school, and mine was chosen. To this day, I still think back to that girl whose legs shook as she made her way to the front of the chapel to receive her plaque. Every time I achieve a new milestone with my writing, I like to think that I'm making her proud.

Through the rest of my childhood, I was inspired by Young Adult authors, those who were writing about the lives of normal teenagers who happened to find themselves on extraordinary adventures. Sure, my adventures were a bit more ordinary, but I knew that I had the words to make them exciting, to make them into something that people would want to read. I started crafting short fictional stories of different genres. I wasn't great at all of them, but they gave me that thrill of creating anyway, so I just did them for fun.

I didn't write much in high school and college, unfortunately. Between the research papers that I had to write and my waning self-confidence, I didn't really have the energy to crank out new material. I got my writing energy out in the grammar units of my English classes, where I pored over my lessons and amassed as much grammatical knowledge as I could. To this day, one of my favorite parts of writing (and translating!) is fully understanding how grammar works and finding the perfect adjective or verb for exactly what I want to say. Josh and I will spend hours on the phone talking about which words fit where in my writing. It's...probably kind of sad how much we enjoy it.

Although I didn't have many opportunities to write creatively throughout my high school and college careers, any chance I was allowed creative liberties, I took them. High school papers turned streams of consciousness, graduation speeches meant to inspire, open letters to people who would never read them, and fictional pieces for creative writing courses in college – any chance I could get to flex my creative muscle, I took.

I've marked every great milestone in my life with a piece of writing. At the end of my high school career, I wrote a graduation speech as well as a guide to surviving in my high school that I left to the next recipient of my locker. When my college invited students to write and deliver speeches for our Baccalaureate ceremony with the theme of "Oh the Places You'll Go" by Dr. Seuss, I simply couldn't resist writing a motivational speech to read to my class. Before I left my first job, I wrote a creative fiction piece using all of the inside jokes my team had during my time with them to give them as my parting gift. When big life changes are happening, my immediate instinct is to document it by writing something.

Toward the end of my college career, missing my writing, I took to BuzzFeed and started creating some listicle community posts. As a busy college student, I struggled to find time, motivation, and focus, so making listicles was perfect for me. It suddenly felt like this was my calling. I just *had* to work for BuzzFeed. I immediately crafted my cover letter and waited for the right time to submit it. Countless rejected applications later, I was still not discouraged. While I may never work for BuzzFeed or another site like it, I know that I'm a good writer. I know that I can use my words to move people, and more importantly, I know that I enjoy doing it.

So, back in 2018, I started my blog. I had let my happiness slip away for too long, and I had let my writing muscle lie dormant. I was finally ready to create again, even if I was afraid to put myself out there. With nothing left to keep me from writing, I had no more excuses: it was time to get back on the horse.

But creating content every week isn't easy for me. Besides having very little time, there's also the question of inspiration. I don't always know what to write about or how well what I write will be received, but I can't get better at my craft if I don't practice it, and I can't get the thrill of creating without, you know, creating. Sharing pieces of myself can be scary, but incredibly rewarding.

Whenever I've found myself struggling to find my purpose, I've turned to writing for solace. I'm greedy for the thrill of creating, and I'm looking for opportunities to write wherever I can find them. It didn't even dawn on me until recently that writing has been this constant in my life, even though I've known this entire time that writing is the one thing that makes me lose track of time. Writing weekly for the blog reminded me that I feel best when I'm writing. So why couldn't I do this for a living? Why couldn't I do what I love?

The problem was that, when it came to the job search, I wasn't using my all-important "whys." I wasn't trying to fulfill my purpose. It wasn't until I started focusing on what I wanted most that I was able to turn my career around and find something that suited me much better.

Unfortunately, my initial attempts to find work as a professional writer were often fruitless because I really struggled to find a job description that suited me. Since I had my blog as proof that I could write regularly (as well as an obvious passion for writing), I knew that content creation was ultimately the way to go, but I still found plenty of reasons that I couldn't apply for certain Content Creator positions. The primary issue was that there was at least one thing on every job listing that involved either a qualification I didn't have or a task I had no interest in doing. Although I wasn't thrilled with the job that I had at the time, I was comfortable with the company, my coworkers, and the work, so I preferred to just stay where I was comfortable than to risk it and apply for a job that I didn't feel was the perfect fit. I regularly checked job postings on several different sites, but none of the jobs ever thrilled me.

At the end of the day, after countless demoralizing and fruitless searches for a Content Creator position that I would enjoy, I would return to the futile task of applying to positions at local colleges, since Student Affairs was something that I had been interested in since my own college career. However, I knew that jobs in Student Affairs were scarce and mainly only open to those who had completed their master's degrees in Student Affairs (which is something I ultimately decided not to do, as I'm sure you remember).

Urged by several people (not just at this time, but throughout my life), I finally bought a copy of *What Color is Your Parachute?* I only made it through a couple hundred pages before I stopped, losing motivation to complete such a large book (as I am wont to do), but what I read was valuable.

What Color is Your Parachute? addresses the fact that you can't have everything you want in a job (or rather, you can, but it's rare and probably shouldn't be your ultimate goal), so you should prioritize a few different facets of jobs in your job search, instead of trying to find something that fulfills all of them. Armed with this knowledge, I knew exactly how to direct my job search. I needed to focus on my "whys." I was attracted to small companies with a friendly, personal culture and a mission that aligned with my passions. Instead of looking strictly at jobs with the title of "Content Creator," I began focusing my job search on those things.

One of the fears looming over me as I continued to search for Content Creator positions was that my creativity tends to ebb and flow. Now that I was determined to direct my job searches to particular cultures and missions, I started to brainstorm missions that I was particularly passionate about. What could I write about regularly without having serious lapses in interest and creative energy? I write my blog, so I clearly enjoy writing about mental health, personal development, and Disney, but I also enjoy writing about topics like polyamory and sexuality. I have also always had an interest in working with startups, and there is no shortage of new startups in the sexual wellness industry, so I decided to redirect my search there.

Redirecting my search to only involve companies in industries that I was interested in completely changed my perspective. I was reinvigorated by the idea of working with and being surrounded by people who shared the same interests as me. Instead of previous jobs where I felt I would have to feign interest in whatever the company's mission was, I knew I would be able to use my genuine passion to create content. Suddenly, the job search wasn't something that I dreaded or a fruitless effort that led to me feeling hopeless. It was now just a series of conversations about things that I loved. This felt right! I was glad that I had pivoted my search to the things that I do for fun.

Now, when I reached out to those in my chosen industry, it was to have an honest and open conversation about the industry and its challenges. I wasn't only interested in a job, but genuinely interested in the newest inventions of the industry. I wasn't looking for opportunities to pitch, I was looking for meaningful conversations.

When you're like me and have a passion for people and meaningful relationships, sometimes "networking" like this can feel a bit disingenuous. For the longest time, I thought that

I had to be some sort of shark to be good at networking, but I'm not a shark at all. If I were a sea creature, I'd probably be more like an octopus or a seahorse (whichever is chiller – the Google search for "chillest sea creature" yielded 0 results). I just have no interest in gaining success at the detriment of others. I'd rather work with the people around me to achieve my goals, not against them.

I also feel like networking has the connotation of using people. As someone who strongly values the human connection and enjoys deep, meaningful relationships, I'd much rather build a strong rapport with someone than only focus on how they can benefit me and my future.

I have found that networking isn't just hovering around the cheese plate or swimming the waters at a networking event in search of proverbial blood. Networking is literally every interaction that you have throughout your day. Networking is bumping into a high school friend at the grocery store. Networking is talking to your parent's friends at a party. Networking is joining Facebook groups and twitter chats with like-minded individuals. Anything that gets you communicating with someone else is networking. I didn't want those I was messaging to feel like I'm a shark trying to sneak my way in. I wanted to get to know them and have an honest conversation. That was the only way to network in true conjunction with my "whys."

Eventually in my search, I stumbled across a Facebook ad for my next employer, and intrigued by their product, I ordered from them. I received their welcome email shortly after, and I immediately knew that I wanted to work with them. Their newsletters were so quirky and fun! They were *real*. I knew that

I could easily create content for them if they wanted someone quirky to help out. I just *had* to reach out to them.

Here's where I point out that I'm a total opportunist. Now, I don't mean the type of opportunist that wants to get ahead no matter what and step on others on my way up the ladder. I mean the type of opportunist who sees potential opportunity, and in a very non-pushy way, goes for it. Back when I was single/poly, I would always ask out people that I vibed with. If I felt we had a connection, I dropped my number. I don't like the feeling of having missed an opportunity. As a freelancer, I am always asking existing clients how I can work for them in a greater capacity. If I see something in particular that I think my client might need help with, I ask them if they would like for me to help them.

So being the opportunist that I am, I reached out to this company with the Facebook ads and awesome newsletters to see if they needed someone to help with content creation. After going back and forth with them and doing freelance projects for them for several months, I officially started working for them full time. I still can't believe my luck.

But then again, I truly believe that manifestation works this way...I finally put my energy in the right direction, and that's when I started seeing results. Once I started looking for jobs at companies with cultures and missions that I liked, I started attracting those companies to me. Plus, the fact that Facebook started sending similar, targeted ads my way probably didn't hurt either. With this combination of being an opportunist and manifestation, I found a job doing what I love.

Everyone has different priorities when looking for a job, therefore not everyone should have the same approach to finding the ideal job. While I prioritized mission and culture, someone else might prioritize job requirements and location. Knowing what you would find to be most fulfilling will be the most useful piece of information when searching for the best job for you. Obviously, there's no guarantee that your ideal job will be available at any given time, but you're more likely to find it when it is available if you're looking in the right place!

And so, the moral of the story is to read 100 pages of *What Color is Your Parachute?* and buy things from Facebook ads! Okay, so not really...but also kinda...

Now that you've seen my "whys" in action, it's time to put yours into action as well. Whether your "why" is helping others, caring for animals, or protecting our environment, it's time to take living your truth to the next level. And most importantly, it's time to CELEBRATE!

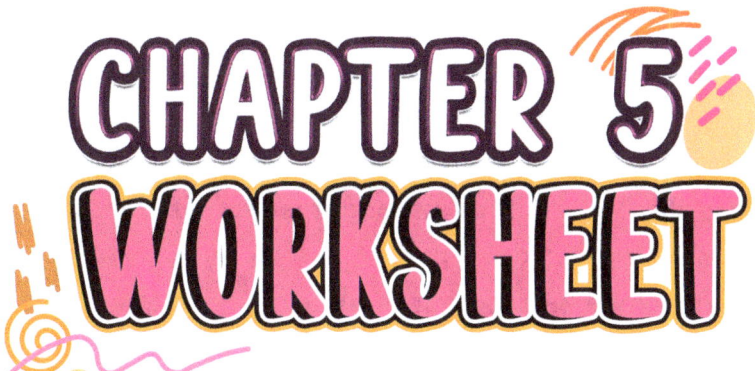

CHAPTER 5 WORKSHEET

Your dream life awaits!

It's time to build the life that you want using your "whys." Are you ready? I know I am!

First, let's rewrite your "whys" right here (you can even add some new ones if you'd like...your worksheet, your rules!):

Next, think of any aspect of your life that you're not loving right now. How can you change to live more in accordance with your "whys" in that facet? Think about all of the main facets of your life and how you can infuse more of what you love in there. Even if it's just one small step in the right direction, what can you do?

In the boxes below, I've put some of the "typical" facets of life that are often discussed. Feel free to remove any, add new ones, etc.

FAMILY

SPIRITUALITY

PHYSICALITY

CAREER

RELATIONSHIPS

(OTHER)

It's a YOU party, and you're invited

Figuring out your "whys" and designing your ideal life is definitely worth celebrating. Now, I want you to think about what else you can celebrate that you've done. And I don't just mean awards you've won. I mean that time that you gave up your seat for the old lady on the bus. I mean the fact that you've started journaling regularly. Maybe you stood up for yourself in a conflict. Either way, you should celebrate each and every victory.

In fact, once you fill out this page, I want you to print it out and hang it on your wall. I want you to celebrate yourself EVERY. DAMN. DAY.

ALL THE REASONS WHY I'M AWESOME...

Self-~~Compassion~~ Celebration Time!

It's important that you think of yourself and your life as something worth celebrating. Treat every accomplishment as though it deserves celebration, no matter how small. Treat yourself as someone worth celebrating. Then, as you build the life that you want, celebrate as it all falls into place.

Making these changes to your internal world can help you change your external world. Once you know yourself and decide the life that you want to live, you can start creating that life for yourself. Maybe until now, you had been trying to bend and contort yourself into a version of you and your life that isn't making you happy.

That ends today.

But it all has to start with *you* and how *you* want to live. Make an active decision today to start living for yourself. And then, celebrate that, too.

OUTRO

The Religion of YOU

NO ONE ELSE HAS to live your life besides you. You're the only person that needs to be happy and feel at peace with your choices. If you live your life according to someone else's rules, sure you might make that other person happy, but you could be miserable. And even if you're not miserable, you could end up living life constantly wondering "what if...?"

What if I followed my own path? What if I chose my "whys?"

Not only do I believe that you should reject other people's "shoulds" in life, but I also believe that you should realize that dictating your own life doesn't have to come down to choosing between only the norm or going against the norm. There are more than two options!

One important thing that I've had to realize in my life is that, while I have the tendency to see much in black and white, there is a lot of gray area. While I might be caught up on the option between buying a house or renting an apartment with my fiancé, I might not even think of the other possibilities like owning a condo, creating a community with different friends and couples that we want in our shared space, or even building a new house of our own from scratch (or plenty of other options that I'm sure exist that I didn't think about – did I just prove my own point with my ignorance? Yes, I did!).

There are certain paths that the majority of people follow, so we begin to see those as the only possible paths. We tend to get caught up in thinking that there are certain ways and certain orders that life events need to happen in order to be "correct." Even going against the "shoulds," we can fall into the trap of very narrow thinking. What can we do about this? Try to "think outside the box?"

I'll do you one better.

There actually is no box.

So many times, we get caught up in the boxes that society creates or that we create for ourselves. Wear a suit and tie. Only work in the field that you studied in college. Work 40 hours per week. Don't be friends with your exes. There are so many preconceived boxes that we allow ourselves to be shoved into. But there's no reason that we can't let them go completely. The boxes don't exist.

Wear sweatpants all day. Choose any career field you like with the hours you want to work. Live with your ex and be best friends. It's your life!

Your internal limitations only go so far as you can imagine. Having trouble removing the proverbial box? Ask a friend what paths they think exist. Ask people who you normally disagree with. Get different perspectives and shed the box away wall-by-wall. Open up your thinking to realize that any traditional and non-traditional routes you can think of can still be limiting. Create the life you want, even if it's not the traditional box life.

Choose to live for *yourself*.

My friend once told me that her mom's last-ditch effort in trying to explain why my friend should believe in God was, "at the end of the day, it comes down to just you and God."

I mulled this bit of advice over, trying to figure out how this fit into my personal belief system. While I would consider myself a spiritual person, I would not consider myself religious. Ultimately, my belief system revolves around the self.

At the end of the day, it comes down to you and...you.

We hear so much about which relationships in our lives are "forever" and which are "transitory" (often romantic relationships in contrast with platonic friendships), but the truth is that all people who come into our lives will change. Some will change and become incompatible with us, some may move away, some may even pass on.

In light of this, it can be comforting to look beyond human connections. Some will choose to look to the divine, and that can be of great comfort if that works for you. For me, as opposed to looking outward or upward, I choose to look inward. When everyone else has gone or forsaken you, you are the only person you have left.

At the end of the day, you have to live with your brain, your body, and yourself, not anyone else. Surrounding yourself with awesome people only goes so far if you're a jerk to yourself when you're alone. So, the most important thing is to be happy with yourself.

That's why this book wasn't about setting goals or making lists or landing you the perfect job/house/life partner/etc. If your internal world is in chaos, your external world will never feel perfect.

Knowing yourself, and maybe eventually loving yourself, helps you to see not only what makes you feel happy and secure, but why those things make you feel happy and secure so that you can seek out more things that feed your "why."

Self-awareness is the first step to everything. You can't find the ideal job without understanding what drives you. You can't find the ideal house unless you know what you want in a home. You can't find the ideal relationship(s) unless you know who you're looking for. Knowing your unwavering core values makes all of these, and everyday life in general, that much easier.

But the most important thing is to recognize that no matter what, things change. Give yourself the grace to change, to go through different life phases. Rediscovering yourself at each new turn is the best gift of all. Don't get so hung up on who you *were* that you're unable to appreciate who you *are*.

You are whole.

You are adaptable.

You are perfect just as you are.

You are YOU. And that will always be the best thing that you can be.

APPENDIX

FUN FACT ABOUT ME: I *love* behind-the-scenes and fourth-wall-breaking stuff. When I find a new thing to become obsessed over, I will Google it to my heart's content, learning everything that I possibly can.

You may not be like me in this way, in which case, you'll probably hate this appendix...in fact, you'll probably feel like this appendix is like *your* appendix, wholly unnecessary and only having the potential to cause pain and suffering.

Or you might just hate that joke I made. Either way, I recommend closing the book here – it's done, you made it, woohoo!

If you are like me in that you love peeking behind that curtain, this appendix is (probably) sure to amuse and delight...or just make you hate me...your feelings are valid no matter what!

There are a few fun facts about this book that I wanted to share in case you were interested.

BOOK TITLE

Back in 2021, I started an awesome job with a unique startup. I learned a lot of new skills and made some amazing friends. For that company, I was tasked with creating a whitepaper out of blog posts that I had already written for the company blog. After I started this project, I started to think that I could do the same thing for my blog. There was an entire untapped audience in the world that didn't read WordPress blogs, after all, and I wasn't reaching them with my writing. On February 13th, 2021, I reached out to Josh to see what he thought about my writing an ebook using some of my blog posts, to which he replied that he had been telling me I should do that since late 2019, about a year after I started my blog. Knowing our relationship, I'm certain he did, and I just brushed him off, believing that what I wrote wasn't worth being in a book.

As we began choosing the blog posts that we wanted to use and creating the worksheets, we routinely checked back to the theme of the book to see if we could come up with the perfect title. We spent hours brainstorming, sent title ideas back and forth, and asked every beta-reader for their thoughts. We just couldn't find a title that worked.

My immediate instinct was to name the book "How to Be Yourself and Not Apologize for It." I also considered "The Religion of YOU," which ended up being the title of the outro. Originally, when I considered writing a book at all (this was probably 5 years ago at this point), the running title was "The Religion of YOU" and it was based on the anecdote at the beginning of the outro.

In fact, the Google Drive folder where I drafted this book is titled "How to Be Yourself and Not Apologize for It / The Religion of YOU." I had no idea what the title would be, but I knew that this was the type of vibe that I was going for.

I asked all of my beta readers to help me brainstorm a title, and while some gave me some great ideas, most of them agreed with me and Josh: titles are hard!

After reading my second draft, Kelsey came up with what would be the final title of this book, "Unapologetic Oversharing, Self-Awareness, and Curly Fries." For someone whose brand is essentially randomness, I loved the idea of narrowing the book's themes down to 3 simple ideas and I loved that one of those ideas was curly fries. As I said earlier, this book would not be the same without Kelsey's help and influence, and her influence begins at the very cover.

Now, I know what you're thinking, that's not the title! Fun fact: I absolutely love curly fries (and have written at length about that love), and every instance where you see Buffalo sauce in this book, it used to say "curly fries." I wasn't sure that I mentioned curly fries enough in the book to warrant adding it to the title, but since my blog is all about Buffalo sauce, Josh and I thought we'd make that small tweak to an already awesome title that Kelsey came up with.

It may have taken us over a year to get this title, but I think it was worth it, don't you?

FOUL-MOUTHED AUTHOR

As is evidenced by the previous point, I do almost everything in life ass-backwards. Surprisingly enough, even though this book didn't have a title, the intro was the first thing that I wrote. While it did help me set up what the rest of the book would look like, I had to go back to the intro to make little adjustments along the way as the book morphed and changed. One point that I made in the intro right off the bat was the fact that there would be cursing in this book. I swear like a damn sailor in real life, and I knew that if I was being true to myself, this book would have some *ahem* colorful language. When my beta readers read the first draft of the book, one of the notes that came back (from my dietitian Kelsey, who gave me a plethora of amazing notes that made the book what it is today) was that there wasn't enough cursing. I had said that I would curse in the intro, so why was there no fucking cursing in the book?

Josh and I decided to make a version of the book with more cursing in it (complete with file folders labeled "Fucking Chapters" and "Fucking Worksheets") and keep one version without the foul language. Then, it came down to deciding where the cursing would go.

One of the strengths of my writing is its conversational tone. Many people who know me personally have said that they can practically hear me reading my blog posts out loud as they read them. I wanted to add in foul language that would maintain this conversational tone and not just throw in curse words willy-nilly. You can't just fuck around and throw "shits" around with reckless abandon, after all.

In order to create the "rated R" version of the book, Josh and I set up a series of phone calls where I read the book text out loud to him, inserting curses where they felt appropriate and natural. This was one of the most awkward parts of the book-writing process, but oh so much fun.

After this was done, I *still* had beta readers come back to me and say that they expected more foul language in the book. Since I thought I had added as much vulgarity as was necessary, I edited the bullet point in the intro. Instead of promising "a lot of fucking cursing," I changed it to "there will be cursing."

Let's not toy with peoples' expectations, shall we?

SHOULD ALERT

The heart of this book is truly that second chapter: *Kicking Should to the Curb*. Since the entire idea of this book is to learn more about yourself, your patterns, and what YOU want out of life regardless of anyone else's expectations, getting away from "shoulds" is key.

When I started writing this book back in February 2021, I really wanted the "shoulds" to jump out from the page and make the reader think. My initial concept had every "should" in the book followed by a bolded parentheses with the words (**SHOULD ALERT**). I wanted it to be jarring enough to make the reader stop and think, but not to annoy the reader and push their attention out of the book. After several discussions, Josh and I decided to abandon this idea, even after considering doing this in other ways such as changing the color of the word "should" or adding an asterisk after each one. While I feel as though this could have been a good way to recognize how often we use the word "should," we didn't want to make the book less enjoyable to read just to prove this point. We just left the apostrophes around all of the "shoulds" (mainly because it isn't a word), and hoped this was enough to make readers consider how bogus most "shoulds" really are.

BUFFALO SAUCE EVERYWHERE

This book, in many ways, is an extension of my blog. Like I said previously, Josh suggested that I work on a book about a year after I started it. Back in 2018, Josh had actually suggested that I start the blog as a sort of digital portfolio. But in this time, it has become so much more than that. Not only have I used it as a robust writing portfolio, but it has become an online journal where I can express my feelings in the present, reminisce about my feelings about the past, and practice one of my favorite things: writing. Through my blog, I've met so many awesome bloggers that have become a wonderful and supportive community for me.

Stop by buffalosauceverywhere.com if you'd like to read more of my inane ramblings (some of them about curly fries, obviously), and say hi! If you're a fellow writer, I'm always looking for guest posters! Being a millennial disaster isn't a requirement, but it is encouraged.

I'll close this out with a quote from "The Breakdown™," my first post ever, the one that started it all (and, incidentally, my mom's favorite post).

"The Breakdown™ is what happens when that little voice in your head tells you that you've let the inertia carry you too far – after years of exciting schooling and moving around where you were dealing with change after change, the changes suddenly...stop. You've settled into a set role that is fairly similar every day. And you start to regret wasting your life away...

...at the ripe old age of 25.

You feel The Breakdown™ coming on as you look over into the next cubicle and your twenty-something office mate is staring dejectedly at her peanut butter and jelly wondering where her life went wrong and your best friend texts you about the tub of ice cream she ate last night without pants on. Yup, it's an epidemic of stagnating young adults. And we're all doomed."

Don't worry, it gets more positive after that. It even ends with a quote from *How I Met Your Mother*:

"Your most exciting days are still ahead of you."

I promise.

PORTRAIT OF THE AUTHOR AS A MILLENNIAL DISASTER

Here is my personality picture from the Chapter 4 worksheet in all of its glory. I really love this picture of me and use it for any bios where a quirky picture fits better than a serious one. It may just look like a silly picture to everyone else, but for me, I can remember the pain I was suffering at the time this picture was taken so acutely. This picture of past Renata reminds me that I can get through anything and that laughter (even if it's at myself) is the best medicine.

Finally, thank you so much for reading my book! I hope that you enjoyed it and it inspired you to do right by yourself. Wishing you a happy, fulfilled future full of comfort.

...oh, and Buffalo sauce. I hope you get to have lots and lots of Buffalo sauce!

ACKNOWLEDGEMENTS

NOTHING IN MY LIFE would be possible without my community.

I'd like to thank my overly-patient, incredibly supportive, and overall awesome editor/ex/bestie Josh. This book would absolutely not have happened without him (only because he helped me start my blog, suggested I write this book in the first place, and dragged me through the editing process until it was complete). But that's really all he did. Now that I've written it all out and reflected on it, he basically did absolutely nothing.

My fiancé Dan who truly believes that I can do anything I set my mind to (seriously, I could tell him that I'm going to the moon next week and he'd just be excited and supportive). My family, who have never hesitated to make sure I have all of the tools that I need to be successful and achieve my goals. Julia, who is not only my best friend and one of the loves of my life, but also a constant pillar of encouragement, empathy, and giggles. My best friend Marisa who is always down to take me out for coffee, build me up with kind words, or vent with me about depression and anxiety, whichever I need most.

My beta readers: Kelsey, Mira, Goeun, Marisa, Kayla, Noelle, Kim, Esprit, Katie, and Kristen. Your perspectives and critiques have truly been invaluable in shaping this book into its final form. My line editor Kathleen who helped me and Josh spot plenty of awkward phrases and misspellings that we wouldn't have seen otherwise (as well as said my tone was a mix of Mindy Kaling and Dr. Sheldon Cooper – NICE!).

So many other supportive people in my life (way too many to mention here) that have helped to encourage and support me throughout my entire life, not just the book-writing process. You've all played a part in each trial and tribulation, and I am truly grateful.

AUTHOR BIO

ENATA IS A MULTIPASSIONATE chronic rewatcher of sit-coms who lives in New Jersey with her fiancé Dan. She's a fierce advocate for mental health awareness and destigmatizing sexuality. When not writing, she can be found doing escape rooms, eating frites at the local ice cream shop, and harassing Editor Josh.

This is her debut book, but if it goes over well, she might write another! Whether or not that happens, you can find her blogging sassily about nothing and everything over at buffalosauceeverywhere.com.

www.ingramcontent.com/pod-product-compliance
Lightning Source LLC
Chambersburg PA
CBHW060536130626
46553CB00002B/781